700 MC

ALCOHOLISM AND DRIVING

ALCOHOLISM AND DRIVING

By

CARL J. BRIDGE, M.D.

Neuropsychiatrist
Keene Clinic, Keene, New Hampshire
Psychiatric Consultant
Franklin Pierce College, Rindge, New Hampshire
Crotched Mountain Foundation, Greenfield, New Hampshire
New Hampshire Hospital, Concord, New Hampshire
Franklin County Mental Health Center, Greenfield, Massachusetts

CHARLES C THOMAS · PUBLISHER
Springfield · Illinois · U.S.A.

Published and Distributed Throughout the World by
CHARLES C THOMAS • PUBLISHER
BANNERSTONE HOUSE
301-327 East Lawrence Avenue, Springfield, Illinois, U.S.A.
NATCHEZ PLANTATION HOUSE
735 North Atlantic Boulevard, Fort Lauderdale, Florida, U.S.A.

This book is protected by copyright. No part of it may be reproduced in any manner without written permission from the publisher.

© 1972, by CHARLES C THOMAS • PUBLISHER
ISBN 0-398-02243-7
Library of Congress Catalog Card Number: 78-187647

With THOMAS BOOKS *careful attention is given to all details of manufacturing and design. It is the Publisher's desire to present books that are satisfactory as to their physical qualities and artistic possibilities and appropriate for their particular use.* THOMAS BOOKS *will be true to those laws of quality that assure a good name and good will.*

Printed in the United States of America
I-2

PREFACE

THE PURPOSE of this book is to utilize the drunk driving arrest as a resource for a study of alcoholism and to clarify alcoholism's relationship to driving. Possible means of improving the current drunk driving problem are considered.

The study was conceived by the suspicion that people arrested for drunk driving were alcoholics.

In a random group of 200 cases, wherein the author determined that the suspects were intoxicated on the basis of a simple neurologic determination, most of whom also had blood alcohol determinations, 173 could be studied in some depth based on availability of background information.

On the Jellinek scale, using the *known* symptoms, all of the 173 cases fitted into either the crucial or chronic phases of alcoholism.

It was once thought that the drunk driving arrest might serve as a means of getting alcoholics into treatment. Interviews were performed in the absence of the arresting officer. Twenty-four of the 200 suspects admitted to drinking problems. Each was admonished by the judge, immediately after conviction, to get help. None did.

The remainder of the 200 suspects practiced much denial. This seemed to be the most prominent feature of the disease. Eight of those who had blood tests said they had nothing to drink. Their average blood level was 0.18 percent (conviction level: 0.10%). Five, who said they had one beer, had a level of 0.21 percent. The stated amount of alcoholic beverage consumed had no relationship to blood level.

Four suspects had been patients of the author. They had seen him for neurotic disorders but had admitted to some drinking. Their average blood level was 0.28 percent as compared to 0.21 percent for the series. This implies that only the very ill seek psychiatric help.

The best sources of information about the subjects are family, friends, and acquaintances. The poorest are local clinical records. There are short descriptions of several interesting cases in the series.

Since this series covers drivers examined in the police station and not in the hospital, many statistics pertinent to accidents cannot be given. However, those involved in an accident showed a somewhat lower blood level than those arrested for manner of operation only.

Because, at least in central New England, nearly all alcoholics are drivers, a number of cases not in the series are reviewed to show the vicissitudes of alcoholism as they apply to driving. Severe alcoholics have managed to stay clear of the law as "lucky" menaces to society.

There is a discussion of how deterioration, from subtle losses of judgment to extreme deterioration, correlate with driving characteristics. Statistics from other studies are cited. New insights into alcoholism are described.

Since alcoholism is not a readily treatable disease, especially without motivation, alcoholics must be kept off the road until there is a definite remission of the illness. Increased availability of public transportation would be helpful.

CARL J. BRIDGE

CONTENTS

	Page
Preface	v

Chapter

		Page
One.	INTRODUCTION	3
Two.	PRELIMINARY OBSERVATIONS	5
Three.	CONDUCT OF THE STUDY	8
Four.	RATING THE DISEASE	15
Five.	REVIEW OF TWO HUNDRED ARRESTS	21
Six.	PRELIMINARY CONCLUSIONS FROM THIS SERIES	35
Seven.	ADDED ILLUSTRATIVE CASES	38
Eight.	ALCOHOLISM AND MENTAL ILLNESS	42
Nine.	ALCOHOLIC DRIVERS NOT ARRESTED	48
Ten.	ALCOHOLICS ARE DRIVERS	51
Eleven.	DRUG ABUSE AND DRIVING	54
Twelve.	INTERPERSONAL RELATIONSHIPS AMONG ALCOHOLICS	57
Thirteen.	STARK REALITIES	61
Fourteen.	THE NATURE OF ALCOHOLISM	64
Fifteen.	HOW TO DEAL WITH THE PROBLEM?	71

	Page
Bibliography	81
Index	83

ALCOHOLISM AND DRIVING

Chapter One

INTRODUCTION

WHO IS THE drunk driver? Is he a normal person whose coordination has been hindered and reaction time increased by rising blood levels of alcohol, in a progression which has been studied many times in the past? But what of his background before a given episode of high blood alcohol level?

In years past a common belief has been that the person arrested for driving while intoxicated is not an alcoholic, but a person who on a relatively infrequent occasion becomes drunk at a party or at a bar and because of his acutely impaired judgment and ability to drive is stopped by an officer or gets into an accident. This view has been fostered by the belief that the alcoholic, because of his vast experience in drinking, has learned to avoid trouble and is just as able to hide his drinking on the highway as he does in public situations and at his place of employment. Furthermore, there has been an assumption by some that the inebriated alcoholic knows better than to drive in the first place. Thus, the poor inexperienced driver gets caught in an embarrassing situation for which he has to pay way beyond the punishment the situation seems to call for, and often a promising young man sees his career ruined because of one indiscretion.

A now defunct attitude about alcoholism is illustrated by a religious tract of about thirty years ago wherein heavy drinking was not as much of a problem as moderate or social drinking because the severe drunk was too drunk to drive or otherwise harm anyone whereas the moderate drinker caused accidents, beat his wife, and so on.

Some classic stories contain concepts of alcoholism which are interesting. In the movie *Lost Weekend* of nearly thirty years ago, the hero, after hospitalization for severe addiction followed by repeated regressions, finally and simply said "good-bye" to his drinking. In *The Old Homestead* of the 1880's, an old man gave a young drunk a ten-dollar bill and *that* cured the latter of his waywardness.

The evangelist Billy Sunday once said of a drunk, "There but for the grace of God go I." Whether that meant that any person can become alcoholic or that he felt the tendency in himself is not clear.

So we see that past concepts of alcoholism related to moral and religious principles. Let us see the scientific concept as defined by the American Psychiatric Association:

> Addiction to or psychological dependence on the use of alcohol to the point that it is damaging to one's physical or emotional health, interpersonal relations, or economic functioning. The inability of a person to do without drinking or to limit his drinking once he starts is presumptive evidence of alcohol addiction.

Drunk driving and alcoholism are henceforth studied together.

Chapter Two

PRELIMINARY OBSERVATIONS

You might ask how the writer became interested in the subject of drunk driving. A psychiatrist has an interest in alcoholism as a behavioral illness. Alcoholism is usually taught to be secondary to underlying conditions. Due to some neurosis, psychosis, or character disorder a person becomes drug dependent. This drug oftentimes is alcohol because of availability and its symbolic bottle of infancy, among other reasons.

This interest in alcoholism as a secondary condition is not only promoted by many psychiatrists and other medical practitioners, but also by other workers in the mental health field such as psychologists and social workers. Because of the lack of knowledge of the basic nature of alcoholism, this still remains in the field of theory. It is my opinion that at times there is such a thing as primary alcoholism.

In the office practice of psychiatry or medicine usually the physician does not encounter his patient inebriated. Even the person who comes in because of an alcohol problem is fairly sober, or at least is holding himself together.

At the time of arrest for Driving While Intoxicated (DWI), however, the subject is intoxicated and he has been pushed into a situation leading to poor self-control because of the trauma of the arrest. The encounter with the arresting officer is a continuing irritation.

In my community physicians are asked by the police to do DWI examinations on a rotating basis. I soon found myself involved in these examinations. Because of my interest in alcoholism I acquired an increasing number of them. Because such examinations are considered a nuisance by most physicians and do not fulfill their real function of treating the sick, my increased participation was most welcome.

The difference in attitude of the DWI suspect as compared to the alcoholic in the doctor's office was obvious. I was also impressed greatly by the evidence at hand of severe emotional disorder at times, and evidences of the chronicity of the alcohol problem. Because of my awareness of the work of Seltzer I had assumed that the relationship of the chronic alcoholic DWI suspect to the total number was about 50 percent, with the other 50 percent, as the public apparently also believed, consisting of poor, unfortunate nonalcoholics who happened to be caught in a rare indiscretion.

It became obvious that the drunk suspect is trying to hide the situation by saying he had just a drink or two and has no alcohol problem. Most impressionable of all has been the ridiculousness of the denials used, seemingly serving no useful purpose. A rational person would realize that stupid denials would hinder his position rather than help it.

For instance, as we have already alluded to, most of the respondents denied having drunk much of anything either on a long- or short-term basis. A few, perhaps inspired by the possibility of getting sympathy, admitted to an alcohol problem. Often there were great mood swings, from being friendly towards the police and others, even jovial, to acting very hostile, making threats, even attacking the officers. Some threatened suit for false arrest. Other examples of ridiculous action included total denial of having driven and inviting people in the police station to have duels.

This type of behavior led to the belief that these people could not be nonalcoholics caught in a rare episode. The person who seldom gets intoxicated would probably retain a fair amount of insight even under intoxication and would not be extremely irrational.

This attitude on the part of the writer, you might say, would prejudice later observations. That is a chance which must be taken, since people who work with people rather than statistics are constantly exposed to situations which can produce prejudice.

In the three years in which I did many DWI examinations prior to the series presented here, I could find no respondent who was definitely not an alcoholic. At the time of arrest, however, there were a few very convincing suspects who said with as much honest appearance as they could muster that they had had only a couple of beers, and that they certainly had no alcohol problem. Then almost invariably this couple of beers produced a blood level of over 0.2

percent, indicating a very heavy intake of alcohol, and when I inquired of Alcoholics Anonymous (AA) people or others around the town who knew them, they were found to have drinking problems.

Admittedly, a person arrested for DWI has little to gain by admitting that he has had a lot to drink, and he would have less to gain by admitting that he had a chronic alcohol problem. While under arrest he might admit to the physician that perhaps he has had a few too many drinks at times. Along with signs of being somewhat intoxicated during the interview, he may look chronically ill and tremulous, and be very fuzzy in memory.

It was especially interesting to note that some of my former and current patients arrested for DWI were among the more intoxicated ones. During their office interviews with me, which most often consisted of just one or two, they often had alluded to no drinking, or they had had some other chief complaint, such as depression, and they drank a little to ease their feelings.

It is the philosophy of many AA members that alcoholism is a disease entity and does not have as its basis psychiatric problems. They point out that the incidence of schizophrenia and other mental illness among alcoholics is no higher than in the general population. I do not know of any such statistics which are valid, so I cannot argue with them.

It is true that many alcoholics are "psychopaths" even when not drinking. However, my belief is that there are some alcoholics who without preexisting psychologic defects outside normal limits have become "hooked" from addiction to alcohol. Perhaps some people have certain biochemical characteristics which predispose to alcohol addiction. Some study has been made of ethnic groups and their incidence of alcoholism: highest, the Irish; high, the French and Scandinavians; lowest, the Jewish. It has even been proposed that if one is Irish, he better abstain!

Perhaps within the next few years a little more will be known about the basic nature of alcoholism. However, direct study of arrested subjects for DWI should add more data to the overall picture.

Chapter Three

CONDUCT OF THE STUDY

You have undoubtedly been wondering what kind of examination is given to determine whether a person is intoxicated and to what degree. In the tabulation of the 200 cases you will note that the suspects are rated as follows: not intoxicated; mildly, moderately, or severely intoxicated. This depends a lot on what might be called judgment on the part of the physician giving the examination. But the determination is based on findings which are at least partly objective.

During the interview there are specific questions asked, such as whether the subject actually drove the vehicle. We have found that this is sometimes denied in a rather foolish way. For instance, the policeman approaches the motorist after the latter is stopped, interrogates and arrests him. Then, later in the police station, the motorist might say that he was not driving because at the time he was approached by the policeman he was not driving.

Then there are questions as to what and how much he drank, when he started and finished, and where he drank. As we shall see, a ridiculous amount of denial is often present here.

Other questions concern general health.

The subject is observed by the physician during the whole interrogation for signs of intoxication, such as slurred speech and disturbed thinking. However, speech is evaluated by such phrases as "Methodist Episcopal," which can bring out some impaired speech which is not always obvious in ordinary conversation. A little slurring can help evaluate the subject as mildly or moderately intoxicated.

The subject is then asked to write something. At times the penmanship is so bad that the subject may be classified as severely intoxicated. More often, however, the writing is almost normal, since it takes quite a degree of intoxication to affect the writing greatly.

The eyes are observed. Watery and bloodshot eyes are consistent with moderate or severe intoxication unless some eye disease or irrita-

[8]

tion can account for them. A person moderately intoxicated will tend to have somewhat constricted pupils. Dilated pupils mean extreme intoxication. The latter is not encountered often in this situation.

The pupillary reaction to light is very significant. Alcohol does slow down the contraction when a bright light is beamed into the eye. There are neurologic diseases which do this, but the suspect will be questioned about possible diseases and they are not common.

The finger-to-nose test is done, with the subject extending his hand and arm, then bringing the tip of the index finger to the tip of the nose with his eyes closed. If the tip of the nose is missed, this usually means moderate or severe intoxication. This is a cerebellar test.

Another cerebellar test is the so-called Romberg. The subject stands erect, with his eyes closed. If he is unsteady he is moderately intoxicated. If he falls he is severely intoxicated. The cerebellum is sensitive to alcohol.

The subject is also asked to do heel-to-toe walking on a straight line. This brings out impairment of gait which is often not seen in ordinary walking. If he staggers on ordinary walking he is markedly intoxicated. If impaired gait is brought out on heel-to-toe walking only, he is mildly or moderately intoxicated.

One other test which is done is picking up coins from the floor. This, in my experience, is not affected to a great degree unless the subject is greatly intoxicated.

From the interview plus this group of tests the degree of intoxication is determined with, usually, a fair degree of accuracy. However, there were subjects with high blood alcohol levels who were able to do quite well in the examination. The opposite of this, doing very poorly with a low blood level, I have not seen in any of my cases before, during, or after the series of 200. This is an interesting observation, since other drugs added to the picture could result in this latter situation.

Conviction in court is based mainly upon the blood level determination. In New Hampshire the critical level is 0.10 percent, as it is in Vermont and many other states. Because of legal technicalities, in order to use a blood level determination in a contested case the technician of the state laboratory fifty miles away must appear in court.

When the technician is unavailable, the physician must testify as to the sobriety of the suspect. It is then on the basis of physical observations that a conviction is made in district court. Where the blood level is "borderline" the physician's testimony is also relied upon heavily. The testimony of the arresting officer is always considered important.

If the case is appealed to a superior court, it is possible that a jury will acquit a suspect on the basis of contradictory or inconsistent testimony. It is hard to predict what a jury will do. While the appeal is in effect, a peace bond can be obtained by the defendant, preventing the lifting of the driver's license until the case has been tried again.

If the suspect refuses the blood test, there is an automatic ninety day suspension of the driver's license beginning with the time of arrest.

It is interesting to note as one peruses Table II, that in spite of some inconsistencies the degree of intoxication does roughly follow the blood level.

Arresting officers have noted that at the scene of arrest the suspect may show a great disturbance of gait and slurring of speech, although an hour or so later in the police station, his coordinative functions have improved considerably. This cannot be accounted for entirely by metabolism of alcohol, because it is disposed of by the body at the rate of roughly 0.01 percent per hour. Thus it would take somewhat over an hour to metabolize an average mixed drink and perhaps two hours for a large can of beer. One can see then, that to have alcohol in the blood over twenty-four hours after ingestion would be infrequent. However, the "quick recovery" described above can be attributed to by some rest and "pulling one's self together."

Just how chronic the case is cannot be correlated obviously to the effect of a certain blood alcohol level on coordination. It is said that the alcoholic who is physically intact and in the earlier stages of the disease shows more tolerance to alcohol than does the person who hardly ingests any at all. This may be so, but it is also noted, especially by AA members, that as the years go by, anyone's tolerance to alcohol decreases, so that a person who has been abstinent ten or more years upon drinking again shows immediately a decreased tolerance, just as if he had been drinking all the time. Young adults should, then, have a greater tolerance than older people.

However, you will note on Figure 1 that the higher age groups have somewhat higher blood levels. This is probably due to a combination of factors. Perhaps it is due largely to the younger individual being more daring in his driving and thus more likely to be picked up.

It might be surmised that even more sophisticated tests of alcoholic influence, such as those which research workers use, involving reaction time, ability to perceive certain stimuli, and others, may give a little more accurate evaluation of intoxication than that obtained in the police station. Considering the many variables involved in determining alcoholic influence, they would probably contribute mainly to knowledge in cases where our examination indicates no intoxication or slight intoxication. As we shall see by the review of the cases, the total life adjustment of the person is very important.

After the on-the-spot data were collected, clinical records were sought locally. Only in a very few cases did they contribute much. Illnesses which could be related to alcohol were found. Alcoholism can be a great imitator of other illness, especially in regard to the stomach and other parts of the digestive tract wherein the symptoms are vague and little or nothing objective is found.

The past arrest records, especially for DWI, can be considered important evidence of alcoholism. Previous arrests for things related

Figure 1
AVERAGE BLOOD LEVELS

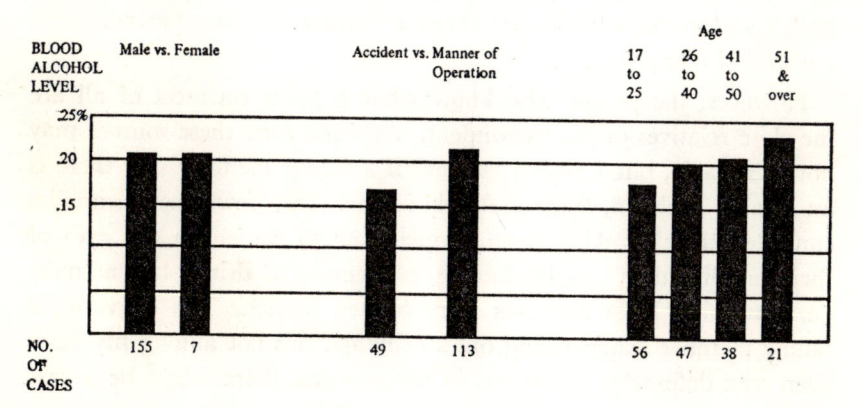

to alcohol consumption, such as assault and domestic quarrels with wife beating, are positive symptoms.

However, this evidence was corroborated by testimony from other sources including the suspect's family. The mere existence of a previous arrest was not considered as determining the diagnosis.

Admission to an alcoholic problem by the respondent was sometimes, but not often, sufficient to establish the diagnosis on the Jellinek scale evaluated on the level of loss of control, loss of jobs, changing drinking patterns, use of technological products, and so forth.

Personal knowledge of the respondent by me, when there was some, was very helpful. The suspect in this case would not necessarily be my patient, but a relative of a patient. As a matter of fact, some severely depressed women who had seen me had alcoholic husbands. In some cases, these women saw me after their husbands had been arrested.

A case in point (No. 17 in Table II) was the husband of a schizophrenic woman I had seen for a few years for control of symptoms, in and out of the hospital. She had described her husband's drinking habits vividly. He was a man prominent in business, and he suffered much from his arrest. Once the arrest is made, it is an accomplished fact, and nothing can be done to reverse the situation.

A close working relationship with alcoholics in remission, active in the community, is extremely helpful. Some of these are in committees active in alcohol education. They seem to have an expert knowledge of who is alcoholic, not just by inference but by meeting these people in AA and perhaps by having them as former drinking partners over a period of many years.

However, the people who know what is going on most of all are the close relatives of the respondent. At times even these sources may not be reliable, but I would say that if a family member says there is an alcohol problem, there certainly is one. In a few cases alcoholics can keep their drinking from people close to them. In the eyes of their families they can be having an occasional drink, but actually be consuming large amounts from hidden bottles. The converse, a family member exaggerating one's drinking, has not among my cases been seen definitely. However, in my practice, there might be a case of a large amount of alienation in a marriage, especially when a man or woman is trying to stack evidence against a spouse in a divorce action, wherein drinking is emphasized. Abusive treatment under alcoholic influence is a common complaint.

When a close relative of an alcoholic is contacted, and a history of uncontrolled drinking is given, corroborative evidence is usually present also, as we shall see. The degree of alcoholism, according to the Jellinek scale, was rated according to the severest symptoms as described by the family or acquaintances, or by personal knowledge of the examiner gained from the patient or public records.

In the cases which are not rated—not all of the 200 could be studied to a great degree—it is because the suspect came from a distant community, and family and associates could not be contacted. With local people and those short distances away, enough resources for determination of degree of alcoholism were usually available.

Even in those few cases wherein the denial practiced by the suspect was shared by family members and others, enough evidence could usually be found to give some rating in the case. At least one person who knows the suspect will admit to the degree of the problem. If the suspect's spouse is alcoholic, there might possibly be the problem of projection, that is, one person attributing his or her own defects on another as an unconscious defense mechanism. However, as stated above, in this series there has been no real evidence that the suspect's habits have been exaggerated by another person.

Returning to the problem of finding local records of a clinical nature, it is noted that in other studies social agencies have been used as corroborative sources of evidence of alcoholism. The exclusive use of such records for rating leaves the numbers of known alcoholics greatly reduced from the actual incidences of the disease, reflecting the paucity of recorded data. Many alcoholics have not come to the attention of any agency because they have not been unemployed, have not abused their children noticeably, and have been able to hold their families together and to stay out of trouble for many years before they are picked up for DWI.

It is interesting that in the case of medical records there will be, at times, a lack of mention of alcohol except for "occasional drinking" or "occasional excessive drinking," but when a practitioner who knows a particular patient well is asked, the answer might be, "He drinks like a fish." The general practitioner often picks up knowledge of drinking from family members, as well as from clinical findings which, as we know, can be sparse.

Chapter Four

RATING THE DISEASE

WE HAVE seen that it is quite difficult to quantitate the degree of alcoholism in an individual. One cannot depend upon physical factors to determine the seriousness of the disease. In the living subject we cannot examine the brain microscopically. Detectable liver disease is a late finding. Perhaps there could be behavioral measurements under laboratory conditions, including neurophysiologic and psychologic measurements, but even these could have grave limitations such as variable degrees of intoxication while measurements are made. Good subjects need to be willing to be studied. Social histories are unreliable because of the hidden nature of so many aspects of the disease. Certainly subjective evaluations are extremely limited in value because of the great amount of denial, which we have seen.

After some search, the only good rating system as to the degree of alcoholism I could find is the Jellinek scale. It was formulated over twenty years ago on the basis of thousands of cases. Some of the categories may not seem to be in the right order, and they may not seem completely relevant, but through the experience of workers the scale has stood the test of time for reliability. Perhaps in the future when more is known about the illness, there may be a new rating scale based upon physiologic factors of an objective nature.

In rating the cases, manner of driving and other immediate circumstances surrounding the arrest were not taken into consideration to be sure that we were not overextending our thinking. It would be very tempting to call very erratic driving "loss of control," or the last category, "rationalization system fails."

One of my first reactions to Jellinek's scale was that the "alcoholic palimpsests" or losses of memory, blackouts or blankouts, indicated a more advanced stage of the disease than his scale indicated. But it is interesting to note that some recent research has pointed out that such blackouts can occur in the absence of alcoholism, even in the nondrinker. This would certainly rate the symptom low, if not off the scale. Undoubtedly Jellinek realized that a person without serious alcoholism can have blanking-out episodes.

In some circles it is felt that blackouts are real warning signs as to the disease becoming serious. I would agree, even with our present state of knowledge, that they are warning signs in that a person getting intoxicated to the extent of having a blankout is in a state of danger, so he should cut out his drinking or make sure that it does not have a chance to advance. To Jellinek, it was mainly a "warning" sign.

As stated at the beginning, one of the big things which prompted this study was the fact that suspects seen after DWI arrests seemed to show signs of rather deteriorated judgment. At times this deteriorated judgment can reach ridiculous extremes as, for example, fighting with the police in the station and making ridiculous threats and boasts.

On the other hand, it is also known that people who have alcohol problems and are still relatively intact can seem very rational and can deny the drinking problem very cleverly. For instance, a person drinking heavily can avoid drinking in the presence of others by using bottles hidden in various places, usually at home, at work, or in the car. Often these people will program their drinking so that they are intoxicated only at a time where there is little likelihood of having to go out to work, visit, or be involved in some social engagement.

Also early in my career as a DWI examiner, I noted self-contradictions. At first I thought that being upset by the arrest situation, which is indeed a traumatic one, could account for such lack of judgment. Who would believe that a person admitting to an alcohol problem had had nothing the night he was arrested?

As you can see from Figure 2, a person arrested for DWI and who had a high blood alcohol level often claimed he had only one or two beers. In addition, he would often say that he drank seldom and he did not see why he was picked up when he did nothing wrong.

This type of denial, one might argue, does not mean necessarily that there is a severe loss of judgment, but that it is the best type

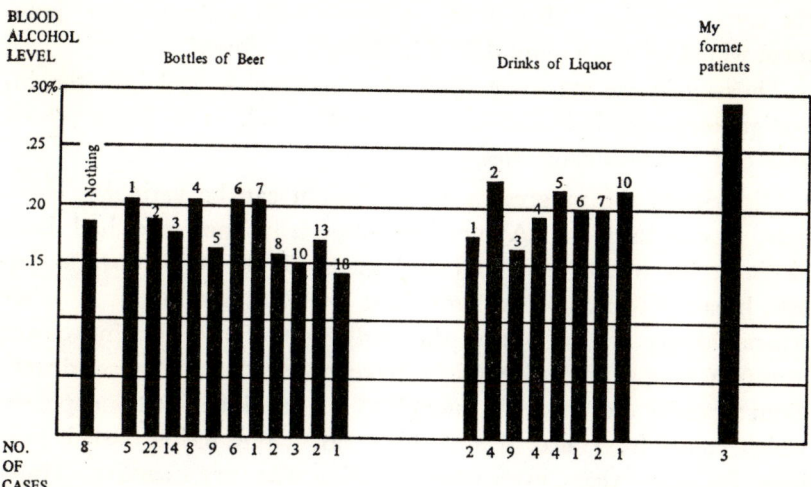

Figure 2
WHAT AND HOW MUCH DID YOU HAVE TO DRINK?

of denial anyone might be able to muster under such adverse circumstances. This may be partly true, but one might also surmise that an arrested individual after the "shock" of the situation is over can regain his craftiness. Law officers can tell you of successful escapes of suspects after they have had time to rest a little and plan things.

Often the type of denial given by the suspect seemed to be very inappropriate to the type and amount of confronting evidence, such as denying any loss of coordination in the face of a very staggering gait and severe slurring of speech. Other examples of losses of judgment which would lead one to suspect a rather serious thought disturbance would be the reason why a person would drink that night, such as trouble at work, a sick dog, or losing at gambling. At times suspects talked of these things in an apparently honest and forthright way, at the same time denying the circumstances he is faced with.

Also very impressive at times was the poor understanding by the respondent of things explained to him. Here again the trauma of the arrest situation could be a great factor but, on the other hand, when simple laws, explanation of rights and implied consent principles were given, he oftentimes did not seem to understand what was said to him or, what is probably more true, did not want to admit he comprehended it so that he could in some way get out of the obligations of the law. Again, one might say that even the person who is not drunk and arrested could put forth rather poor defenses against the arrest situation. More likely, a person with undeteriorated judgment would be much more skillful in defending himself.

Thus again we see some signs of things which lead into the investigation of the individuals, which finally result in his being placed in one of Jellinek's categories.

Histories of the progression of alcoholism can be variable. However, if one talks to AA members, especially ones who had been alcoholic for many years and had gone all the way down to job loss, breakup of family, skid row and complete destitution, a rather typical history is that during the early part of the drinking career it was a happy time. He might have been called a happy drunk. Even when he did not drink enough to get drunk he felt the euphoria which comes from alcohol and this good, happy feeling lasted, perhaps, for many years, even when drinking was very excessive. However, it might seem that to maintain the euphoric state the drinking could not be excessive all the time. Nevertheless, he might talk of the good companionship, parties, wonderful adventures, and give anecdotes about what others did when they were drunk. It all sounds as if it is a story of great happiness at first.

Sooner or later troubles creep into the picture. Because drinking is a progressive habit, it is finally maintained on a very steady basis, starting with a drink in the morning.

When this stage is reached, where there must be some alcohol in the body all the time, the glow, the euphoria, has gone. Sometimes this is discovered suddenly. Now he is drinking, but the happiness is gone. As he looks back on the whole picture, it is hard to remember the progression of the alcoholism; it is hazy. But then the stage of real drunkenness has been reached. The person is drunk all the time and is miserable. On the other hand, he is afraid to breathe a sober breath.

This undoubtedly sounds paradoxical. As we have and shall see, there are many contradictions in this whole subject of alcoholism. For instance, an alcoholic has to drink because of inner tensions, yet when he is drunk he shows more tension than he does while sober. Anyhow, when the alcoholic finds himself drinking much of the time and feels sick, he is afraid to be sober because when he is sober he will feel the tension of wanting a drink again and he knows he will be shaking, more nauseated and nervous. He is caught in a box.

You might ask at this point, at which stage of this scheme of things is the drunk driver? Is he still in a happy drunk stage? We know that he is more than "prodromal" in the Jellinek scale. He is at least "crucial."

In the experience I have had interviewing the suspects, a few have seemed euphoric or carefree, as a designation on the examination sheet describes. He might agree to anything done at the police station and not show any open resentment to the arrest. It must be remembered, however, that these people, as well as the openly resentful ones, denied the drinking problem as a rule.

It was also interesting to note that in some cases where people put on a carefree and happy attitude in the police station, this was sometimes intermingled with crying and sobbing for short intervals when the importance of the situation got through to him or her.

It is when the alcoholic gets to the point of being sick all the time that he is brought to the hospital for care. Then he goes into delirium tremens or at least severe shakes. If he tries to go "cold turkey," stopping drinking without the help of drugs, the withdrawal is worse. Rarely delirium tremens (shaking, with extreme irritability, confusion, and seeing objects such as small animals) are handled with the help of friends and AA members for a few days, the AA members being "baby sitters."

After a drying out period, the drinking is often resumed, for a variety of "reasons." More often than not the alcoholic will have good intentions after drying out. But the weakened personality cannot yet tolerate the frustrations of daily life. He reacts to those frustrations with the attitude that he might as well give up completely, that he does not care and nothing matters, so he starts drinking again. Sometimes drinking starts again when things seem unusually good and he feels that since the thing has been licked, why not have a drink? Perhaps the unconscious mechanisms in these situations are similar, but they certainly return one to excess once more. Healing from alcoholism is a long process.

In Table I those cases which could be rated are tabulated. Please keep in mind that they are categorized according to the most seriously known symptom in each case, the actually most serious one probably worse. In the tabulation in Table II each studied case is also rated according to the Jellinek scale.

Chapter Five

REVIEW OF TWO HUNDRED ARRESTS

From Table II, the following cases are selected for brief discussion because of their being "typical" yet showing special points, worthy of note.

Case 2. This man, as you can see, had no blood level of alcohol tabulated. At the time of this arrest he refused to give a sample. He admitted to no alcohol problem, but he stated that he had been picked up for DWI two days before he went into the service. The blood level, 0.15 per cent, was slightly too low for conviction under the old law. That had been five years before this arrest. At that time he claimed that he had one or two bottles of beer, and he had been classified as slightly intoxicated on examination.

His local clinic record told of much adolescent behavior and psychosomatic pain. For a long time he was on Librax®, a tranquilizer and antispasmodic designed to relieve gastrointestinal spasm.

A year after the arrest listed here he was again arrested for DWI and was found on examination to be "possibly under the influence." I did not make that examination. His blood level was 0.22 percent and he was convicted.

During a conference with a prominent AA member, the latter classified this man as having been in "bad shape a long time." My informant told me how this man has been consistently, almost daily, openly intoxicated, had lost many jobs, and had been drinking obsessively. His court record, as tabulated as arrests on the table, were mostly, if not all, arrests for disorderly conduct and fighting in association with drunkenness.

Case 6. This respondent was quiet and cooperative during the examination. He was found to be markedly intoxicated. His blood level of 0.20 percent was actually a little lower than expected. He said at first that he had no drinking problem, that he merely had a couple of drinks before going to bed each night. The night of the arrest he claimed that he had five Scotch whiskeys with soda at a local cocktail lounge. In the conversation after the examination, he continued to say he had no alcohol problem. Finally he said, half-heartedly, "I guess I have a problem." He pleaded guilty and the judge gave him an admonition to seek help, but he never did. His wife was contacted by telephone. She said that he drank compulsively every day, especially in the evening, but he was always able to keep his job. At the time she was contacted, his arrest had not changed his drinking pattern.

Case 10. This man submitted to the usual examination except for the blood level. He was quiet and withdrawn, but he did not seem unusual insofar as intoxicates are concerned. He stated that he had had three beers that night. Locally, he had a clinic record which mentioned asthma and emphysema. There was no mention of mental illness. However, it was found that in another city he had been arrested for DWI two years before. He had acted so psychotic at the time of the arrest that the charge had been dropped and he had been committed to the state hospital where he stayed for two months—diagnosis: schizophrenia, paranoid type. At the time of the arrest I was involved in, he was at large under a bench warrant for a defaulted appearance for a traffic offense. His mother was consulted. She stated that he is all right when he does not drink, but when he does, which is much of the time, he gets very withdrawn, almost silent, and has crazy ideas, such as believing that there are people after him.

Case 12. This person had been seen by me in the hospital in delirium tremens after many years of heavy drinking. I saw him in my office once on a follow-up basis, but he failed to keep his second appointment. The DWI arrest I saw him for was a little over a year later. On examination, he was moderately intoxicated, but his blood level of 0.35 percent should have put him in or near coma. He said that he had had three beers. There was, later, an admonition by the judge, with no result. Knowledge of this case was based largely on his history as I knew it.

Case 16. This woman was arrested for erratic driving. She admitted to having had some whisky but she did not know how much. It was interesting to note that over twenty years before, she had been jailed for assault and battery, and over ten years before, for disorderly conduct. Around the same time she had lost her driver's license for a few months because of an accident involving property damage. She had not been arrested at that time for DWI.

On examination, the amount of intoxication was judged as moderate. She admitted to having had an alcohol problem in the past, but not at this time since she drank only on weekends and not during the week when she worked. Her local clinical record showed only a skin condition.

Since she had admitted to having had a drinking problem, the judge advised her to get help. Apparently she did not, and she continued drinking. Her death from cirrhosis was less than a year after the arrest.

Case 23. This man was from another state, over five hundred miles away. He said he was in this territory on vacation. He claimed he had no drinking problem whatsoever at that time and he never did have any. He also said that during the evening he had had two beers only. After the examination I decided that his case would be of no help because he was too far away from home for me to obtain any correlative data. After the examination a local man called and said that he was a fellow AA member of the subject, and he was coming down to post bail. It turned out that the suspect was staying at a nearby drying-out establishment. Information from a colleague who serves that drying-out home helped me determine that the suspect suffered from extreme lack of alcohol tolerance, and he was definitely a chronic alcoholic.

Case 44. This person was arrested for an accident, wherein he sideswiped another car. He was asked whether he was the operator. His answer was, "I might have been and I might not." When he was asked where he started out from, he answered, "That's for me to know and you to find out." He was asked if he had any illness. He said, "Yes, I have a sore finger two months." He did not cooperate with the examination, refusing to do most of what was asked, but his speech was very slurred and he staggered. The most prominent observation was that he was very filthy—skin and clothes were caked with dirt. Although he refused the blood test, he admitted to having a little problem. In requesting the judge's admonition I commented that he would soon become a derelict if nothing were done for him. About a year later he was committed to the state hospital because of alcoholism. He had been picked up intoxicated, with no visible means of support.

Case 52. This was and is a local business man of some prominence. He was very angry at the arrest because he said he "drinks like this only once a year." That night he claimed he had only five whiskys with water.

Because he was half in a snow bank he fought the case both in district and superior court, claiming that he was off a public way.

According to his clinical record, a year later he was treated for moderate injuries sustained in an auto accident—no DWI accusation at that time. Later, he had hepatitis.

His wife admitted that he had been drinking steadily for a number of years, but that in the previous year or two he hid his steady drinking, but it got out of control more often. Although his progress in alcohol consumption was not known clearly, he was still drinking three years later, and he had been promoted in his organization.

Case 61. This man was was arrested on his way home from a wedding. He claimed he never had an alcohol problem. Since by this time I realized that all the DWI cases I had studied thus far had turned out to be alcoholics if pertinent data were available, would this case ruin my 100 percent statistic? He was an out-of-stater. He stated that he had had three or four beers only, but he was moderately intoxicated—the old syndrome. It turned out that a local AA member knew this man well. He was known as "a real alcoholic" who had drunk obsessively for many years. This man had spent time in a state prison because of injuring a person in a fight while drunk.

Case 68. This young man sat sullenly in the police station shortly after he was arrested. He was well dressed and composed, but he was obviously angry. He answered very few questions, and he refused to be examined fully. His pupils showed a poor reaction to light and his eyes were watery and bloodshot. His gait was poor and his speech slurred. He had been picked up because of slow driving and weaving. This was a second offense.

It was learned from one of the arresting officers that this man had been an undercover agent with a governmental department investigating drug traffic and a variety of other illegal activities. He had lost that job a few years ago because of another DWI conviction, and now he was a private investigator.

He fought the case both in district and superior court, and lost. I had to testify both times. My own investigation in the community in which he lived revealed that he had for nearly five years been an ineffective individual because of drinking which was uncontrolled, and it seemed that a few drinks made him act irrationally. This man had refused to discuss any drinking problem. People who knew him stated that his habit went on after his appearances in court.

Case 82. This man refused his blood test because eight months previously, he claimed, he had been arrested for DWI after having had only two or three beers, and the blood came back "19." Therefore, he claimed, that test had been false and he would never have another one. He said, "I do have a chronic alcohol problem. I've been so drunk I couldn't stand up, but not that night." His wife stated that he drinks heavily every day. He admitted that his memory is very poor. His arrest record covered about five years. The admonition from the judge led to no help, as usual.

Case 90. This subject was followed by the police because he was driving his truck erratically. After he was stopped and got out of the truck, he accused the officer of dating his wife. When I saw the subject he was extremely excited, antagonistic, and disoriented. His wife stated that he had been drunk three weeks. Because he was so out of control, he was committed to the state hospital that night. He was kept at the hospital only three weeks. His case was classified as alcoholic hallucinosis. It cleared up in a few days, but he was kept for a period of rehabilitation. When last heard from a few years later, he was drinking again.

Case 146. This man admitted that he had been in the state hospital when he was interviewed. He had been picked up for driving on the wrong side of the road. He claimed that he had had six Rye whiskys with gingerale. Some time later, as I was investigating the case, I found in his local clinical record that four months after the arrest he was sent to the state hospital—diagnosis: schizophrenia. My own notes at the time of arrest quoted him as saying "I was nervous ever since I was born." His commitment resulted from his having been apprehended putting up flags in inappropriate places while playing music loudly on a radio. He had been drinking. His family reported that he lived only for his next drink.

Case 159. This man was found asleep at the wheel of his truck. However, he was picked up because of two complaints earlier in the evening wherein the police had been informed by telephone that the truck was weaving all over the road. When first interviewed he claimed that he was not driving because he had too much to drink to drive, that he did all his drinking in the truck, then fell asleep. When he was confronted with the fact that he had been observed driving very shortly before he had been found, he denied having drunk anything at all. A close acquaintance of his informed me later that he drank very heavily and regularly, before and after his arrest.

Case 160. This twenty-seven-year-old man was stopped because he was weaving all over the road. He claimed that he had had only two bottles of beer. His rather severe state of intoxication seemed a little, but not too, inconsistent with his blood alcohol level of 0.22 percent. In other words, this case seemed to me a mild exception to what is generally true, that most suspects have an expected or higher than expected blood level. After the examination, when I attempted to engage him in a conversation about his problems, it was obvious that his speech was very unproductive. At times after I put questions to him he gave no answer, but he looked at me as if he did not know what I was saying. At other times he gave slow, short answers devoid of any depth. When asked whether he had an alcohol problem, his answer was "Yes and no," and he would not elaborate. His actions were very reminiscent of chronic schizophrenics who have much blocking of thought and speech. However, in his case his demeanor was more characteristic of the slowing down or psychomotor retardation which is seen in depressed people or ones who have had certain types of brain damage. So in addition to the usual denial one sees in this situation, there is some evidence of deterioration. His clinical record showed only an examination when he become a city employee, and a city employee he was, a common laborer who managed to do shoveling and other odd jobs. He was not married. People who knew him described him as being some kind of zombie who was not really "with it." It seemed that he drank some all the time, but his mind had not seemed clear at all in recent years. An AA member described him as always being in "a lot of trouble." The record in Table II certainly confirms this. A few years later he was in relatively the same state.

Case 163. This man was retired, divorced, and had a very long history of both alcoholism and depression. He had been in mental hospitals and drying-out institutions intermittently for the previous thirty years, and he was employed by drying-out places intermittently as an attendant. For the previous few years he had apparently been dry. I had seen him for depression, and he was treated successfully, seemingly. A few years before I had sent him to the state hospital because he was found collapsed in his apartment in a very disoriented state. It was while I thought he was in an abstaining phase, well dried out and working diligently at an alcoholic drying-out home, that he was arrested because he hit a meter in a parking lot. A few days later he was on his way to the hospital again. This person was an interesting one in that despite the insight gained by his working with alcoholics many years, he often slipped, whenever he felt depressed to the point of not caring what happened. Also, once he started drinking he showed extreme memory loss, disorientation, and even hallucinations, so that each time he hit bottom it seemed that he had undergone permanent brain damage, and he would spend the rest of his life under custodial care. However, on each occasion, after he had been dried out, he seemed to regain all his mental faculties. As far as I know, after the arrest episode a few years ago, he has remained dry ever since. This man had a very severe depression which was haunting him for many years and must have had a lot to do with his turning to alcohol many times. On the other hand, working in very active alcohol rehabilitation programs did not give enough insight and motivation to keep him away from alcohol. Before his retirement he was a very skillful business man. We were not dealing with a stupid person.

Case 167. This young man was picked up for erratic driving. At the scene of arrest, when asked to stand he swayed, and he had a hard time standing up. He claimed that he had had two bottles of beer and one shot of whisky. He did moderately well on the examination at the police station. His blood level of 0.12 percent was too low for conviction under the old law. Under the present law 0.10 percent would result in conviction. He did not admit to any alcohol problem. It would have been easy to eliminate him from the series, but as no arrest was arbitrarily dropped from the series of cases, I decided to "see it through." His clinical record showed that he had been treated for minor injuries when he hit a dog with a motor cycle. He had also been treated for vague abdominal discomfort, paravertebral strain, and asthma. This man was a mild mental defective who came from a large family wherein mental deficiency was very common. Since this family was known to me, I made some inquiries and found that this person had been drinking quite heavily. His pattern was such that he went on long periods of drinking rather heavily, and then he would not work. Then when he was out of money he would drive a truck for a while until he got enough money to drink for another prolonged period. He lived with his parents and had no one to support.

Case 169. Although this man refused his blood test, he was willing to talk to some extent. He refused to state how much he had to drink on the evening of his arrest. He claimed that he has only two beers per day except for rare occasions when he "drinks once in a while at home." He refused to elaborate on what he meant by that, but I construed it to mean that he had days of drinking at home much of the time. The interesting thing about this case is that at the time of arrest I did not recognize him, but in reviewing his clinical record I found that six years previously I had seen him as a neurologic, not a psychiatric patient. He had been arrested for threatening a man with a gun. He had severe headaches and loss of memory. Although he showed no physical signs of increased pressure inside his head, he was referred to a distant medical center for a neurosurgical workup, especially to rule out brain tumor. Locally, at that time, there were none of the usual diagnostic tools for such an evaluation. It is noteworthy that drinking was not mentioned in the clinical record, although one might surmise that it had been gone into and that the usual denials had been made. A year later there was a letter written by another physician to the state motor vehicle department stating that the subject was again fit to drive. Examination of his police record revealed that his previous DWI arrest was just prior to the gun threat episode, and the two events led state authorities to want him off the road. Subsequent investigation revealed that this man had for several years been drinking very regularly, without any dry periods. His wife stated that he seemed to have had to consume a certain large amount of whisky each day and larger amounts on weekends.

Case 172. Although this man came from a distant community, it was a city I visited about once a month. He admitted that he had had three mixed drinks that night. Actually, three strong mixed drinks could produce the blood level of 0.10 percent which he had that evening. Although he was picked up for erratic operation, he did quite well in the examination where the degree of intoxication was classified as mild. This case also could have been excluded from the series rather easily, since he could not have been convicted at that time because of his low blood level of alcohol. However, despite two DWI convictions and three convictions for offenses associated with drunkenness, he stated that he never did have an alcohol problem. He also claimed that prior to this evening he had had no alcoholic beverage for about three months. Some time later I made inquiries in his community. His mother offered the information to the effect that he had been a steady drinker for the previous three years, with no periods of real sobriety, and that on weekends his drinking tended to become relatively heavy. A doctor in that community also knew this man as a steady drinker. Here we find, then, a young man well on his way to severe alcoholism. His being from a distant community was a handicap to being involved with future follow up.

Case 173. This man represents one of the more blatant cases of psychopathology. You will note that the degree of alcoholism was not rated, even though I had a lot of personal familiarity with this case. The fact is that this person even while sober exhibited much poorly controlled behavior. He quit jobs very frequently and on impulse. He was often getting into fights. It was a fact that he was sober for some periods during his life because he spent much of his time in houses of correction. He came to me briefly for psychotherapy as a court referral, because it was hoped that with help he could improve his behavior. Unfortunately, he drank on impulse as he did everything else. He was very angry the night he had his accident. Presumably he had gotten into an "I don't care" attitude because he was going at a very high rate of speed, and he slid off the road at a curve and rolled over. After his examination he complained of chest and arm pain, so he was admitted to the hospital later. He had no fractures. His state of intoxication was extreme, even though he claimed he had only two glasses of beer. He continued to be angry as he was admitted to the hospital. During hospitalization he had no withdrawal symptoms because he had not been drinking for any length of time. After the acute effects of alcohol left him, he seemed quite depressed. It was felt that his depression was secondary to the emotionally unstable personality. Psychodynamically, the anger which was ventilated outwardly while he was drunk was now directed against himself. He had enough insight to realize how much of a mess he was making of his life, but he lacked the control to improve himself on his own. He was transferred to the state hospital for further care. Since then his adjustment has been improved, but just how much so is difficult to say.

Case 176. This man's alcoholism was what could have been termed common knowledge in the community. His four previous convictions on DWI charges were on the basis of very obvious intoxication. He was picked up for weaving on the road, and his intoxication was very marked. He had nothing to lose by refusing the blood test, since he would lose his driving privilege indefinitely anyhow. He claimed he had only six glasses of beer that night. Although his clinical record mentioned nothing about drinking, around fifteen years prior to this arrest he was treated on two separate occasions for contusions and abrasions suffered in falls. Those who knew this man described him as a very heavy drinker over twenty years or more, with some changes in his patterns of drinking, at times drinking secretly, and in other periods drinking openly, and at times seeming sober for periods of time yet carrying the odor of alcohol. The rating in this case would, with more intimate knowledge of this person, probably be much higher than the one actually listed, but, for the sake of accuracy, the highest symptom definitely known is given.

Case 177. This case represents a young man who was unfortunate enough to have a two-car accident, but he was not hurt. He was arrested because there was some odor of alcohol at the scene. On examination, there was no evidence of intoxication. He said that he had two bottles of beer. Two large bottles could produce such a blood level. In this random series this case could have been disposed of very easily as being a "control" or a nonintoxicated driver. After all, driving after having had a couple of bottles of beer is not a very unusual circumstance. His clinical record revealed, however, that during the previous ten years, while he was a student in junior high and high school, he had multiple falls and bicycle accidents. He also had complained of headaches, but no pertinent physical findings were ever uncovered. He had never been evaluated psychiatrically. An investigation revealed that members of his family characterized him as a steady, fairly heavy drinker for long periods of time, with some periods of sobriety between. This latter picture does not definitely correlate with his arrest situation, but by inference we might say that his accident took place in the early evening (as it actually did) when he had started doing his nightly drinking, and that his bad driving was the result of more chronic factors related to drinking.

Case 178. This case is interesting because it involved a snowmobile as the vehicle driven. In response to a noise complaint the police investigated and found the subject driving around on the road in a very carefree manner, disregarding traffic. However, when the police car started flashing blue lights he could have taken off across a field and escaped, but he did not. The case became a small sensation. Several acquaintances of the subject said that his life revolved around his drinking, that he drank a "fair" amount on working days and always to excess on days during which he did not work. One person who knew him well stated that he seemed to revolve all his activities around drinking, even such sports as snowmobile driving. The suspect said he had no idea how much he had to drink that night, but he definitely had no alcohol problem and he never did.

Case 180. This man had several phobias and he acted as if ridden with anxiety. He had been picked up for erratic driving. In my conversation with him after the examination he said, "I have a drinking problem, but I want no record of it." His conviction was made on the basis of a urine examination in lieu of blood, because he was terribly afraid of needles. Reports of urine testing are made as equivalents of what blood testing would show. He admitted to having had six bottles of beer. It is interesting to note that he had a local clinical record with several entries in it by physicians who were not psychiatrists. One called him an "odd personality complex" but did not go into detail, except to say that he had "no depth of purpose." He often went to doctors with stomach aches which improved with Librax® and Carbrital®. In his many visits to physicians there were other complaints, but no definite physical findings. Because of his stomach complaints he once had a GI series, which was negative. In none of the entries on his record was there any reference to alcohol consumption. This may well have been because he denied it. At any rate, alcohol is a common cause of gastritis. Stomach symptoms are always to be regarded as possible signs of alcoholism.

Case 198. This young man claimed that he never had an alcohol problem and that on the night of arrest he had had nothing to drink. When it was pointed out to him that his driving had been erratic he denied that there had been anything wrong with his driving. After the examination, I had a conversation with him during which time he admitted that once while drunk he rolled a car over, but the accident was never reported, and he got away with it. Still, he said, he never had an alcohol problem. He just got drunk once in a while. Investigation of family and acquaintances revealed that this man was a very regular drinker. He had lost some jobs because of absenteeism after bouts of drinking heavily, but all the time he was drinking on a regular basis also. His family believed that hardly a day went by when he did not have something to drink. At times he seemed to be in fair control of himself, but on many occasions he seemed to be mixed up, and then his main purpose was to get his next drink to straighten himself out. However, even during his good periods he seemed to require alcohol to avoid tremors and anxiety.

Case 200. This man started as my patient about three years prior to the arrest under discussion. This forty-eight-year-old man had been seen by me in hospital consultation while he had delirium tremens (DT's). According to his medical history, he had been in them once before, five years previously, and his history of alcoholism covered at least twenty years before that. It had allegedly started during World War II. He drank very heavily as a soldier, but he stayed out of trouble and advanced in rank during his term of service. After his honorable discharge, he soon married the girl he had been engaged to before he had been drafted. He had cut down his drinking considerably shortly before his marriage and for a few months afterwards, but soon his drinking had become uncontrolled. Five years later, after having had two children, his wife had divorced him because of abusive treatment while he was drunk. A later marriage had also ended in divorce. The hospital admission I was first involved in had resulted from another doctor having found him in his home drunk after a request for a house call because of suspected pneumonia. That was not the case. After he came out of the DT's he claimed that he never really had a drinking problem and that for the past several years he had abstained completely. He was advised to come to my office for follow-up visits. He never did so, but about two years later he was again in the hospital with DT's. This bout was almost fatal. Afterwards he admitted in a rather uninspiring way that he guessed he had a drinking problem, but he would never drink again. Then he did come in for office therapy a few times. He claimed that he was abstaining from alcohol. He also claimed that he was very depressed. He was living alone, having been divorced, and he had no interest in anything. He was despondent. In the therapeutic situation an attempt was made to interest him strongly in something other than just his job. I felt that the therapeutic relationship at that time was excellent. He seemed to gain some genuine positive feelings. However, after a time he came to the office smelling of alcoholic beverage, and he had slurred speech and a staggering gait, but he denied drinking at all. He missed an appointment, and then I did not see him again until about three months after his last episode of DT's, when I was called upon to see him for DWI. When I saw him in the police station he said he bumped a car accidentally while driving from a friend's home. The police said he was driving on the wrong side of the road. He claimed that he had been abstaining. At this friend's house he had what he thought was two drinks of pure ginger ale. This friend, he said, is a severe alcoholic (he certainly is), and he was at this friend's house to stop him from drinking and to join AA. My examination revealed mild intoxication but, as you can see, his blood alcohol level was very high. When he appeared in court he pleaded guilty, but he said he must have been slipped whisky without his knowledge. As far as I know he is drinking heavily still.

Chapter Six

PRELIMINARY CONCLUSIONS FROM THIS SERIES

THE MOST striking fact to be seen in this series is that all subjects who were actually drunk drivers were alcoholics falling into either the crucial or chronic stage, according to the Jellinek scale. Also, as we have seen in the case discussions, some of those who could have been dismissed from the series as not being, technically, drunk drivers at the time of the arrest turned out to be alcoholics.

The next very important fact (although not tabulated on Table II) is that apparently none of the subjects arrested for DWI sought professional help for his alcoholism as the result of the DWI arrest. Those who admitted to having a drinking problem and even asked for help at the time of arrest (only two subjects), and then being advised by the judge to get help failed to seek assistance of any kind, in the first few months after arrest at least.

As to the behavior of those arrested, the big theme which has been mentioned many times and will be discussed again is that of denial; denial not only of the alcohol problem generally but of the immediate circumstances leading to the arrest. It is true that this is a situation which calls for denial as a defense against the attack on the individual's self-esteem, in the form of the arrest. One might say further that since there is no good denial available, the mind chooses a stupid one as the only one available, especially since the brain is poisoned with alcohol.

Another interesting subject which we have encountered is the relationship of mental illness to alcoholism. You will see in Table II how some of these subjects were schizophrenics and others had character disorders and psychosomatic illnesses. The series of 200 is really too small to form a clear statistical relationship between alcoholism and other disorders, but these cases we have gone over certainly tempt one to make definite connections.

It seems, however, that the person with mental illness would be more apt to turn to "sedativism," which alcoholism has been called, as surcease from inner anxiety, and so set up a condition wherein alcohol addiction takes place. We have mentioned to some extent how some theorists claim that all alcoholics have some kind of significant defect to begin with, before they become addicted. What our study does not show is whether or not this is true, because the early personalities of the subjects are not known, as is the case in other studies. We shall go into that later, also.

A conclusion which we can make justifiably is that people arrested for DWI should certainly not be drivers as long as they are drinkers, and they should be kept away from the driver's seat until their mental faculties are clear.

Perhaps most of the case reviews left you "hung up." Stories we read usually do have some kind of ending. Fairy tales have, "They lived happily ever after." Tragic dramas leave the dead hero in a state of sad glory. But these cases, I am sure, most often have left you in a state of unsatisfied limbo, as they do me.

You probably have noted that a few of these people were dead within a year or two after the arrest. A few are apparently dry, probably not as a result of the arrest directly, but because of some later motivation.

Generally speaking, those who are still around town and are well known are still drinking, getting into trouble occasionally, and deteriorating, presumably on a chronic basis.

I often hear rumbles about alcoholics still drinking, ". . . but not like they used to." That is a phenomenon which requires a great deal of research and discussion as to whether it actually exists very often, and, if so, how it manages to take place. Apparently there are alcoholics who manage by dietary discretion to stay alive without serious deterioration and to pass through middle age without becoming totally abstinent but settling down to drinking less. AA principles are definitely against this, partly because these alcoholics in partial remission flare up into fatal episodes. But there are enough of the "burned out" alcoholics around to establish this as a possible entity. They are people who have suffered severely from their disease, yet seem to settle into a level of adjustment wherein they still work, keeping some control over themselves, and drink to some extent. Some of these manage to drive without getting into trouble, and others have given up driving.

A significant number of DWI subjects have left the community. This fits in with Jellinek's concept of changes in location, "geographic escape," as one of the symptoms of alcoholism.

The lack of positive results from admonitions of the police, doctor, and judge to seek help and get the alcoholism treated is the discouraging aspect of the whole situation, but it points out the reality of the alcohol problem. Alcoholism is a most difficult disease to say the least. We shall have to seek new ways of attacking it.

Chapter Seven

ADDED ILLUSTRATIVE CASES

THERE ARE a few cases of DWI which were not included in the random series of 200, but which are narrated here to underscore further some of the vicissitudes of alcoholic intoxication. These show some of the more extreme cases of mixed up thinking and troublesome circumstances surrounding alcoholism.

This particular incident occurred about two years prior to our tabulated series of cases.

A fifty-five-year-old man arrested for DWI showed on examination extreme alcoholic influence. He was hardly able to stand up. His blood level was 0.26 percent. During questioning he said he had had no alcoholic beverage whatsoever, just as some of the subjects in our series claimed. He was also asked if he had any alcohol problem, or whether he drank at all, to which he answered "No." He said he never had any alcohol problem. He was then asked whether he had any illnesses. He answered that he probably had some nervousness. He stated that he saw a certain local surgeon. When asked why, his answer was "alcoholism." Certainly this surgeon had no time to deal with alcoholism in depth. This person was on Librium®, a tranquilizer often used by alcoholics to relieve tension which would result in drinking. Often it is successful. Many AA members are opposed to the use of tranquilizers totally, with reason. Often the alcoholic uses the tranquilizer correctly. Then, if he slips and starts drinking, he finds that the tranquilizer augments the effect of alcohol. This subject did just that with Librium. Later, the surgeon was contacted. Apparently this doctor had recognized this person as an alcoholic for many years, but he refused to go to anyone else for help. At times this man abstained, and it may well have been the case that the tranquilizer was what enabled him to stay away from alcohol for periods of time. After the arrest this man did not seek further help, at least for a few years.

A commonly seen circumstance is illustrated in the case of a twenty-eight-year-old man who was stopped for a minor traffic infraction; going through a stop sign without stopping completely. This happened about a year after the series of 200 cases. As he was apprehended and checked, it was noted that the interior of the car was filled with the odor of alcoholic beverage. The arresting officer had him walk a straight line heel-to-toe at the scene of the arrest, and it was felt at that time that he was somewhat under the influence of alcohol because of slightly slurred speech and some apparent inability to walk straight. The strong beer odor was the main factor leading to the arrest.

About three quarters of an hour later, at the police station, I found that he did very well on the examination. He walked the straight line almost perfectly. He did not sway while erect with his eyes closed. He performed the finger-to-nose test well, and his speech was not slurred. My impression of him was that he was slightly under the influence of alcohol, because even though he did well, I had the feeling that he was not quite up to his normal self.

Because this man had a blood alcohol level taken, and it came back 0.16 percent, which at that time was only slightly over the level required for conviction, he was brought to trial, and I was asked to testify as I am when the defendant contests the charge. I thought that it would have been better for the prosecution had I not been called upon to testify, since my observations were favorable to him. The prosecuting attorney was impatient, even somewhat angry, at my testimony. The laboratory worker who processed the blood testified and, as a result, there was a conviction. The case was appealed to Superior Court, but the defense dropped the appeal just before the trial was to take place.

This subject had the reputation of being a heavy drinker for some time.

This was one of several similar cases encountered by me, wherein the blood level was much higher than anticipated. In a DWI examination performed by one of my colleagues, there was a man who did very well in the police station but his blood alcohol level was 0.26 percent, which one would ordinarily think of as causing an advanced degree of intoxication. This case was fought in two courts, with a resulting conviction.

As far as the opposite situation is concerned, having a low blood alcohol level along with signs of marked intoxication in the cases of DWI I have seen, well over 500, I do not recall anyone as having a much lower blood alcohol than expected at the time of arrest.

This latter picture would be expected where there is the influence of other agents augmenting the alcoholic intoxication. Other examiners have seen this situation.

The above case illustrates how, when a person is not grossly deteriorated from the effects of alcohol, he can pull himself together for some time in a way which allows him to keep his drinking in secret, if that is his intention. It allows a large amount of denial insofar as his basic problems are concerned.

This is particularly true of young people who have not yet had much time to become deteriorated. Young adults do not seem to have a great tendency to stop eating when they drink. The older, more advanced alcoholic stops eating when he drinks heavily, usually. The young person is more efficient neurologically. The middle-aged person who shows signs of advanced alcoholism has probably drunk heavily in his twenties and the more obvious ill effects from it have not been seen until he reached his forties, when drinking interfered greatly with his eating. Certainly many of you know of young people who put away almost unbelievable amounts of whisky for a number of years before signs of deterioration took place. Perhaps you saw them staggering about and getting into their cars to drive home. Those who are relatively overt about drinking are, perhaps, people who are extroverted, such as salesmen, or are psychopathic in their behavior, acting mainly on impulse, while those who are defensive, even paranoid, will be more likely to be secretive about it.

The latter case is exemplified by a man who had a heavy drinking problem which he was usually able to control to the extent of staying out of trouble. Once, when he found himself in a state of having had too much to drink, he decided to drive very slowly and carefully. The police, who knew him and the car, knew what the situation was. He was found to be intoxicated, with a blood level of 0.24 percent. He was angry, almost justifiably, because he had not violated any traffic law. His driving was very careful and accurate.

Police are on the lookout for that type of driving. Actually in our series in Table II "erratic driving" never included that overly slow, careful driving that alcoholics sometimes perform. Obviously, in an emergency situation, the intoxicated driver, although extremely careful, would be impaired in his coordination and reaction time.

Chapter Eight

ALCOHOLISM AND MENTAL ILLNESS

At this point I wish to return to a consideration of those in Table II who were my patients, plus some study, in a general way, of others who have come to see me as patients. You will note in Figure 2 that the cases there had an average blood alcohol level much higher than the average of the whole series.

All but one of these four cases came to me because of severe alcohol problems which they admitted to. Obviously the number of cases is not statistically significant in any accurate way, but some interesting observations and inferences can be made.

First of all, these people had seen me relatively early in my career in Keene, because they were nearly at the ends of their ropes. They represented cases wherein the usual alcoholic denial had been broken down sometime before.

When people are not accustomed to having psychiatric help in a community, the people seeking it do so on an emergency basis principally, as contrasted to that which is the case in large cities where it is a common practice to see a psychiatrist for what would be thought of as ordinary neuroses long before breakdowns would occur.

These patients of mine were actually former patients, ones not seen by me currently at the time of arrest. This meant, and this is borne out by my personal review of the cases, that they stopped treatment when they enjoyed only a partial remission of their symptomatology except for one case wherein he stopped treatment, then went on drinking and practicing his alcoholic denial.

These people, while under treatment, which was rather short and of an emergency nature, reached the point of obtaining some relief of their symptoms and withdrawal from alcohol long enough to recoup themselves temporarily and then resume their drinking.

This very small group of people who had sought out psychiatric help does not seem to be very convincing evidence that psychiatry has much to offer people with very severe alcohol problems, on the face of it. However, rather than concluding the latter I could certainly rationalize in a different direction and say that since these people sought help only on an emergency basis, they were not motivated for psychotherapy which would lead to a major change in life style and some change in personality. These are the usual goals in psychotherapy.

These people, who were not in any sort of longterm, regular psychotherapy points out that in the field of psychiatry, unlike that of any other medical specialty, there must be very strong motivation on the part of the patient if real treatment is to be attained. A person with a bad sore throat or even pneumonia who is not particularly inspired to get medical help, but still manages to make it to the doctor, can be cured of his malady by use of antibiotics and other short-term drug administration. In psychiatry, the situation is very different. It is true that psychiatrists under very short-term circumstances help people out of situations and perhaps even effect changes in persons in one or two visits, but this is usually not the case. Considering psychotherapy in a person with a long history of alcoholism, wherein it has reached the point of being life-threatening and there is a real emergency situation, the person must be dried out for a while until he gets to the point where he can really be reached. As AA people will point out, the recovery from alcohol is a very long one, and the "moral" recovery is longest of all. What is referred to as moral has to do with the finer discerning functions of the brain, free of the gross denials and distortions, which must be utilized if there is to be any really meaningful psychotherapy. So, we require some weeks for real drying out, and if there are underlying problems which need treatment, psychiatric sessions are planned over a period of months.

This may seem to represent an attitude of hopelessness. The disease is not hopeless, even though the cure rate in alcoholism does not seem high. But it is high enough so that one should not be totally pessimistic about the outlook. No matter how dark the picture is, unless the alcoholic is in the process of dying of medical complications there is always some hope.

Apparently where hope is the poorest is in the case of character disorders. These constitute a large part of the realm of alcoholism. The presence of a major psychosis, or insanity, makes the outlook poor. We reviewed Case 146, which one could think of as a schizophrenic whose symptoms were brought out more by alcohol. Case 173 represented a major character disorder, whose course did improve.

The presence in the alcoholic of the so-called alcoholic personality, which had led to the overt illness of alcoholism, has been argued pro and con for many years. Statistically, there is little help in proving or disproving the concept. As we have seen, many people, particularly AA members, contend that the presence of emotional and mental illness is the same in a random sample of alcoholics as in the general population. However, for many years the American Psychiatric Association has used the designation "Sociopathic Personality Disorder, Addiction Alcoholism." This does not mean, absolutely, that the person involved had a preexisting personality disorder before he was a practicing alcoholic. It does mean that once a person is addicted to alcohol he has a personality which is sociopathic or psychopathic.

Psychopaths, a terminology no longer official, are people who act mainly on impulse. They do not profit by their mistakes. Their feelings are not deep in a lasting sense. Their attachments to people, or to anything, are not lasting. Their feelings are very changeable. However, people who are sociopathic or psychopathic often have the appearance of feeling very deeply about things. Then they change so rapidly that it appears that the previous picture never really existed in the first place.

A classic example of this is a case of a young man who, after having made many mistakes involving stealing, embezzling, etc. talks to his counselor very logically, admitting to the errors of his ways, and saying that he is going to lead a new life on a more rational basis. He is very sorry for what he has done. Then on the way out of the office he steals something, leaving never to return, and goes on in his sociopathic way of living. These people do not, as a rule, commit major crimes which require planning, but are involved in nuisances such as fighting, sexual impulsivity, and spur of the moment larceny.

These people are excellent salesmen. They could sell someone the Brooklyn Bridge, or the moon. They tend to make very good initial impressions on others. Glib alcoholics can do this when they are not very intoxicated.

The fact that these people do not learn from their mistakes makes sociopaths and alcoholics much alike in at least one respect.

Insofar as driving is concerned, this poses a severe problem. A person who is a sociopath or represents a psychopathic personality can do things at the spur of the moment. A psychopath I knew suddenly decided to drive her car into a cement wall, and thereby kill herself. There are similar cases I know of. Certainly such judgment can be lethal to others also.

A case of interest is one not in our tabulated series, that of a man whom I saw only once. Believe me, these psychopaths do not make good office patients because they cannot be depended upon to show up for their appointments. Because he was really over a barrel—he had lost his driver's license because of reckless driving, and he felt greatly anxious because he had lost his job and was in a lot of other trouble—he came for immediate help, at which time a program for therapy was set up. He never returned.

He continued to work for some time, on a new job, after having miraculously escaped jail for assault. He continued getting into trouble because he was short tempered. He got into fights easily, and he did other spur of the moment acts such as walking out on the woman he lived with, staying away a few days at a time, not showing up for work, etc.

One night he became intoxicated and he became very angry at something his living partner said. He drove her car away. At that time his driver's license had been suspended for two years. In this intoxicated state he drove on the wrong side of the road, hit another car head on, killed himself and an occupant of the other car, and injured severely the other two occupants of the other car.

We can see readily what problems can arise with alcoholics, especially psychopathic ones. Certainly the only way to keep alcoholics off the road is to take away their licenses. If this does not deter them from driving, the only other alternative is continued incarceration. The problem is a very bad one, because it seems that if anyone with any kind of difficulty involving alcohol is going to be rehabilitated he must be taught to live as nearly normal a life as possible, but if on the spur of the moment he gets a completely "I don't care" attitude and decides to drive, there is not much to stop him.

In police records, driving after suspension of a license is a common offense. Whatever the answer to this problem will be, it will not be easy, since bans on driving are not easily enforced. They cannot be enforced without making some innocent people suffer, since, if this were carried very far, one could be kept off the road unjustifiably for minor or unproved infractions.

It is true that some, but not all psychotic people should be kept off the road. Some schizophrenics have been known to run down pedestrians because voices have told them to do so. Depression and anxiety affect driving. However, not all troubled people should be kept from driving. There are some well-controlled schizophrenics who have excellent driving habits, and there are neurotics who drive very well. Their driving privileges should certainly be based upon past performance.

The confusion that can exist in the relationship of emotional illness to alcoholism can be illustrated in the following case.

A forty-six-year-old man came to me because of nervousness and depression. He was an apparent success in the appliance business. He had been hired as an assistant to a man whose business had been failing. The patient had rescued it and had been doing very well. However, his sales started slipping and he admitted that he was somewhat addicted to phenobarbital. He was taking over fifteen tablets per day from old prescriptions.

He gave a history of having been a severe alcoholic for several years, having almost reached the skid-row level. After he had finally gotten into a drying-out program and AA, he abstained, and he continued to abstain for the next fifteen years, he said. However, depression seemed to plague him all his life, and he believed it had started his alcoholism. Several months before I saw him, he found that phenobarbital gave some relief, but recently he felt sure that the increasing dosage was making him forgetful, so he was referred to me.

I withdrew him from the drug gradually and put him on an antidepressant and tranquilizer. Almost immediately his boss and wife complained that he was very shaky, forgetful, and mixed up. At first that was understandable as possible inital side effects of medication, but continued use of antidepressants and tranquilizers is associated with the disappearance of side effects. In our sessions we dealt with depression. Since no one suspected him of drinking, and he denied it strongly, this was not considered a present factor. However, his work performance did not improve, even though he claimed he was less depressed, and he lost his job. When that happened, he checked into a drying-out establishment and admitted that he had been drinking. In retrospect, in our sessions he seemed to bring up several things about drinking, such as how he knew a man in a drying-out home who was very active in alcohol programs and was dry for many years, after which he drank and soon landed in the local cemetery. Now the patient is working again. Drinking? I don't know. His old boss still is.

Chapter Nine

ALCOHOLIC DRIVERS NOT ARRESTED

THIS CASE, as several others, will be presented to illustrate further the vicissitudes of the alcohol problem. It may sound as if I am harping on one theme, deception, to excess, but it is a most important theme. It is amazing how people can be fooled, including those who are allegedly familiar with the problem.

Several months ago I was asked to see in consultation a man who had been doing some construction work. A brick fell on his unprotected head. He was knocked unconscious for a very short time. How long was not documented. It could have been momentary, or as long as several minutes. After this incident he had a typical post concussion syndrome. This can happen even after only momentary unconsciousness. He felt nauseated and light-headed, and he was unsteady on his feet. He also had a little dull headache.

He tried to go back to work for a few days after the accident, but because of persistence of symptoms he had to go home and lie in bed. His wife said he also had personality changes. He became much more irritable and unreasonable.

Because of the slight possibility of a slow hemorrhage in the head causing a deterioration of his condition, he was admitted to the hospital for study. He had negative skull x-rays and a negative neurologic examination, except for a little unsteadiness of the eyes. His electroencephalogram, or brain wave test, showed some evidence of concussion.

He was directed, upon return home, to stay at relative bed rest, getting up only to eat and to go to the bathroom, until he could tell subjectively that his symptoms were improving, and then he could increase his activity according to his tolerance. After he could walk around for a sustained period without weakness and nausea, he could drive his truck and bulldozer for a very short period of time.

In two months the brain wave showed complete recovery from the concussion. However, his wife complained that his actions had become even more bizarre. He became more demanding and unreasonable, and he did childish things, such as picking fights with the childern, kicking the door in, and storming out of the house on many occasions.

It was only at this point that a past alcohol problem had been admitted to. Then his wife said that before his head injury he drank heavily, but he started abstaining about two months before the injury. She was sure he had had nothing to drink since the accident, since she found no hidden bottles, and some partially full bottles in a cabinet were undisturbed for some time, several weeks. There were also no real signs of intoxication. This last myth was exploded one night when he came home openly intoxicated. When he finally abstained, he recovered from the concussion symptoms completely.

Another interesting case, involving driving indirectly, is that of a forty-five-year-old man who came to my office complaining of depression. He had typical symptoms of depression including sleep disturbance, lack of interest in things, inability to concentrate, feeling low and dejected, actually having crying spells, and sexual impotency. He said that he had been drinking a little to fight his depression, but drinking was not really a big problem. He said that he felt the same whether he drank or not.

He was treated with antidepressant medications with some success. Before he improved completely he got much worse for no apparent reason. The depression returned.

His wife volunteered that he had been getting intoxicated frequently recently, and actually he had been drinking heavily for a long time.

He was referred for treatment to an alcoholic drying out home. He spent a week in the infirmary, during which time he was somewhat tremulous. After this he spent a month in the guest house with the AA program.

It is worthy of note that once his treatment for alcoholism was well under way he was not on an antidepressant or any other medication. At the conclusion of the treatment program he had no symptom of depression whatsoever. For many months thereafter, perhaps to the present time, he remained abstinent, without symptoms of depression or any other neurotic disease.

During his illness, he had been driving frequently and "normally."

I might mention at this point that my private patients *during* treatment for alcoholism and alcohol-related problems were driving and were not arrested for DWI. Many drove throughout their alcoholic careers, I am sure.

A forty-eight-year-old woman, who had a history of being dependent upon methamphetamine for dieting and keeping awake, yet was obese, and chlorpromazine for her restlessness, was admitted to the hospital because she was found on the floor by her husband, with right-sided paralysis. Her speech was slurred, but both she and her husband maintained that she did not drink at all. Her paralysis cleared up with a little persuasion, but a day later she went into delirium tremens. She almost died in that condition. She was discharged from the hospital two weeks later.

A month hence she called her physician. Her speech was slurred and she claimed she really had a stroke this time because she fell down twice. She was found to be intoxicated upon admission to the hospital. She was transferred to the state hospital for long-term treatment of her alcoholism. This took place over the vehement protests of her husband, who claimed that she had been abstaining completely. This patient drove nearly every day she was not in a hospital. Her record was perfect—no arrests and no accidents.

This case again illustrates how extreme denial can be. But it brings up another point; namely, how people close to an alcoholic participate in the denial at times. In some cases, as we have seen, the alcoholic actually hides the habit from those close to him successfully for periods of time. I have also seen, in other cases, where the denial is participated in under threat, usually threat of death, great bodily harm, or abandonment. This often takes place also in cases of drug addiction. In this particular case the real cause of the denial on the part of the husband could not be determined definitely. It is a fact, however, that the husband had a history of alcoholism in the past, but was apparently abstaining, according to the wife, around the time of this episode. Since then, the denial had continued.

Apparently the only successful enemy of denial is objective evidence, such as blood alcohol levels. Even then, denials persist to the **bitter end!**

Chapter Ten

ALCOHOLICS ARE DRIVERS

THE LAST CASE in the last chapter was that of a woman who went through all of her alcoholic career, at least as long as I knew it, with a perfect driving record. Let us elaborate.

A fifty-five-year-old man had a thirty-year history of excessive drinking. He never had medical treatment until his wife noted that he ate very little and he was losing weight. This man owned a small construction business. After having a few drinks for breakfast he continued drinking during the day while working. He drove home from his jobs so drunk that often he had to be helped from the car into the house by his wife. Finally, his malnutrition became so severe that he was hospitalized. He had become almost as a skeleton and his liver was enlarged. It was at the point where he could no longer walk unassisted that he was admitted to the hospital. He went into delirium tremens and died. His driving record, legally speaking, had been perfect—no accidents or arrests.

Here is a short case illustrating how alcoholism involves driving.

I saw in consultation a fifty-four-year-old man with an old war injury which had caused a chronic osteomyelitis, a bone infection, which was being treated at a Veterans Administration (VA) facility. He used his pension money to drink, as many pensioners do. There is nothing an alcoholic would like better than to continue his habit with some money he does not have to work for!

One day he collapsed in his very dirty room, and he was taken to the hospital quite drunk. He recovered from his acute alcoholic bout quickly. He should have been retained in the hospital for much further treatment and in anticipation of delirium tremens. He said, however, that he *must* get to the VA hospital for an important appointment. Arrangements were made, and he was dispatched with a note requesting that he be retained for the treatment of his alcoholism as well as his chronic infection.

A few hours after he left, I received a call from a surgeon at the VA hospital saying that my patient had arrived to see him without an appointment, drunk, and the ambulance driver who brought him was also drunk.

He was promptly returned home, but in a few days he was readmitted to the local hospital in delirium tremens. He recovered from that episode, but he is now dead, from aspiration of vomitus.

One thing I have learned through years of experience is that when an alcoholic in a hospital has just sobered up and he *must* be released for important business, that important business is the next drink!

It is fairly obvious that the drinking public consists of driving drinkers. This especially hits home in central New England, which is semirural, and in which public transportation is practically nonexistent. This makes almost every adult a person who has a driver's license and one who actually drives a good part of each day. Commuting to work is by car except in a few cases where the worker lives within walking distance of his factory or other place of business, which is comparatively rare.

Carrying this to a logical corollary, one might say that nearly any patient who has seen me about alcohol problems has driven to see me, and most patients who go to publicly supported alcohol clinics drive there unless they have already lost their licenses, which is often the case. Likewise, people drive to and from their places of drinking, or they drink in their car, if they are not drinking at home.

Admittedly a few alcoholics I have known have willingly given up driving because of their drinking. They are few indeed.

This poses a real dilemma. One can conclude that clearing all the alcoholics off the road would cut down the accident rate tremendously and the fatality rate even more. It would be an economic boon. Insurance premiums would be lower; so we see that drunk drivers affect all of us, not just the very unlucky ones whom are run into by them.

What would be a good answer to this problem? Certainly a man has to support his family, and his wife or others often cannot be depended upon to get him to work. Car pools have been a help to those who have lost their licenses.

Increased availability of public transportation would be a great help. Having a drunk on a bus or train is obnoxious, but not lethal. In the big cities where public transportation is available and it is difficult to keep an automobile, almost everyone is forced to rely on subways and buses. Perhaps you have noted on a trip to a big city that it seemed as if nearly every bus or subway car had at least one inebriate on it. There were probably others who had been drinking heavily but were not overtly intoxicated.

One might assume that a solution to this problem might be the addition of public transportation to every community. This is very expensive. Passenger transportation is almost always uneconomical, including even the systems who have full loads. Reduced insurance rates would have their savings nullified by increased taxes. However, increased public transportation would cut down on automobile use generally.

We must keep in mind that an alcoholic who does not need to drive often does so. In a few of my DWI cases a sober person has offered to drive for a drunk and was vehemently refused by the latter.

Have you ever considered also that perhaps drinking might increase a desire to drive? It has been said that an automobile psychoanalytically represents a powerful penis. One is needed when alcohol produces impotency.

Chapter Eleven

DRUG ABUSE AND DRIVING

Rumors from other cities have it that there has been difficulty in convicting drunk drivers because it turned out that their blood levels were far too low for them to even be brought to court. There was allegedly some evidence of drug use in these cases.

Occasionally blood barbiturate concentration is determined along with blood alcohol level. Unfortunately, many state laboratories do not have the capability of detecting in the blood the presence of commonly abused drugs such as marijuana and the various hallucinogens.

In the series of cases presented here, plus all the others I have seen at the time of arrest, there was no clear evidence of drug abuse contributing to the intoxication. In a few cases where there was especially bizarre behavior this was suspected.

A case I was familiar with, involving an arrest elsewhere, is worthy of note.

A twenty-three-year-old man had a very long history, with a familial one, of uncontrolled anxiety. He needed large doses of a phenothiazine tranquilizer plus a barbiturate in the form of amytal sodium. Such a regime on the face of it might seem injudicious, but it was found that this was absolutely necessary in order to render him functional at work and in the rest of his life.

Earlier in his career there was an interesting situation. He could not sleep well, and he asked for the use of paraldehyde, which he had had previous experience with. He was given a prescription for about 10 cc at bedtime, as a sedative. Paraldehyde is a relatively safe drug which has been on the market since the last century. It was widely used in the treatment of alcoholic states before chlorpromazine (Thorazine®) gained widespread use.

This man was picked up for DWI because of erratic driving. An alcohol blood level was determined as 0.05 percent, which showed that he had had a little to drink, but he could not be convicted on a DWI charge. When his blood level determination came back to the police they apparently became somewhat angry, and they modified their charge against him and served him with a new warrant, which they claimed they had a right to do, driving under the influence of a controlled drug. Since the drug could not be identified, the case was dismissed. As a matter of fact, the judge did not even bother to comment.

I found later that this man had overstocked and overused his paraldehyde, and he was undoubtedly getting somewhat intoxicated from it. Fortunately he was able to be withdrawn from it. At the present time he is making his marginal adjustment on sedation and tranquilization. He is working steadily, but he has some trouble with interpersonal relationships. He tends to be seclusive. He is not definitely psychotic, but he probably represents a borderline state, which is near psychotic. He is constantly troubled by anxiety, which seems to be a family trait.

In and around this city of 20,000 there have been many "busts" for possession and sale of illicit drugs. There was a case of speeding, wherein the college boys involved threw some marijuana out of the window of a car before they stopped. Erratic driving was not involved. The marijuana was found and they were convicted of illegal possession. They were not known as habitual drug abusers or "heads," since their drug use had not affected their performance at school in any detectable way.

Since there is widespread drug abuse in the community studied, and it apparently never came up as an issue in the convicting of a DWI case, it might be inferred that the commonly abused drugs do not affect driving very much. I do not believe this is the case. I would certainly hate to see some of the people I have observed on bad trips at the controls of a car. It may be, and probably is true, that young people under the influence of drugs avoid driving more than they avoid trying to fly out a window. However, certainly there must be young people smoking marijuana at the wheel in lieu of tobacco.

Getting stoned on marijuana has inherent limitations which the use of alcohol does not. Marijuana and amphetamines would affect judgment and reaction time but would not produce the erratic driving which would lead to a DWI arrest.

It is well known that amphetamines have been used by truck drivers for the purpose of keeping themselves awake. Amphetamines, although they make people feel alert, affect adversely motor functions and judgment.

It is also well known that sedatives and tranquilizers, which have sedative side effects, do cause sleepiness and can bring on the type of accident which sleepiness ordinarily causes. Sedation causes increased reaction time and could in extreme cases cause erratic driving.

Barbiturates and other sedatives do increase the effect of alcohol. Tranquilizers also enhance the effect of alcohol. In none of the cases under consideration was this found to be the picture, however, although this situation has certainly not been ruled out in every case. It is a fact that alcoholism and drug abuse coexist. Alcoholism itself is a kind of drug abuse.

The almost total preponderance of alcoholic driving over "drug abuse" erratic driving would lead me to the conclusion that, as serious as the drug problem is, the alcohol problem far overshadows it in importance.

Chapter Twelve

INTERPERSONAL RELATIONSHIPS AMONG ALCOHOLICS

In the previous descriptions of individual cases, it seemed as if alcoholics inwardly are loners. Their addiction is indeed an inner problem, an inner need for a chemical which in advanced stages is an all-consuming need. However, we have also seen in our general considerations that early in the course of alcoholism there is a stage wherein alcohol consumption is associated with happiness, even fellowship. Early in the illness, alcohol use seems in many cases to bring one closer to others and the rest of the universe, just as those who take psychedelic drugs feel that they have opened avenues of communication. It is true that people who lack confidence in the company of others can gain that confidence through use of alcohol, and the drinker feels friendlier, generally closer to others. We have also considered that this euphoria and fellowship can go on for years before the unhappy state of feeling drunk and sick take over. Then, as with any illness, more primitive dependency needs become pronounced, and the alcoholic leans on others in an infantile way.

We know that alcoholics band together to battle the problem in the AA organization. But do alcoholics band together for common protection and help during their drinking careers?

Mutual invitations to parties and get-togethers might be considered a mutual aid to drinking.

In the case of DWI arrests there has been some evidence of help for the suspects by other alcoholics; ones who come in and post bail and try to influence the arresting officers in some way. This was not a very frequent occurrence. Usually monetary and legal help came by way of family members.

However, one might surmise that drinkers have group identifications which are conscious and unconscious, just as people identify in groups according to religion, ethnic background, and profession or trade. Even their alcoholic character formations can become a basis for group identification. Most of all, they drink together.

At the risk of sounding extremely paranoid, there is a question which could be brought up. Could there actually exist an organized undergroup of alcoholics?

When one has been threatened with complete ruin by an influential alcoholic, during a DWI examination, one might wonder whether an organization will be after him.

Could there be such a thing as an "Alcoholic Mafia"? Some people with paranoid tendencies, especially the strict prohibitionists of years past, thought that such a thing did exist. Certainly among some political organizations such as the local Irish Democrat groups there could be a sort of brotherhood of drinking partners, not to mention some lodges. That certain social cliques of drinkers, as we have considered, exist is certainly not imaginary. Many alcoholics have told me that their greatest stumbling block in a program of total abstinence was that all their associates drank and they had no abstaining friends or business associates at all.

It could well be that on a nonofficial basis these drinking associates can do favors for each other, some on a secretive basis, and that there could be sort of a network of special favors, such as army medical officers supplying other officers, usually of higher rank, with medical alcohol and whisky in exchange for food, clothing, and promotion.

It is very dubious whether such drinking association could be on a highly organized, underground basis. It is known as a fact that some men with serious alcohol problems are being retained by their business organizations for longer periods of time than they would be otherwise because their superiors are men who have alcohol problems, and so comradeship and identification with each other exist.

However, a house divided against itself cannot stand long. For instance, it is a widely known fact that marriage to an alcoholic is never pleasant. It is also known that when both partners in a marriage are alcoholic they get along less well than when only one is alcoholic because the husband and wife find themselves fighting over the bottle, hiding it from each other, and so on. The relationship degenerates to that of a couple of quarreling children trying to outdo each other. This sort of competition among alcoholics can start fights at parties and barrooms. A man who does not take his proper turn in buying drinks is inviting trouble.

Alcoholics can become very paranoid about each other and argue about seducing each other's wives. Personal insults produce serious fights. Alcoholics also use projection on each other—the "other guy" is the drunk.

So I would conclude that business associations between alcoholics can be a source of suspicion and hostility. This, of course, would prevent any highly organized activity among people under the influence. It is also obvious that people addicted to alcohol lose their integrative and creative powers, so that obviously an advanced alcoholic is not an efficient cloak and dagger expert.

However, we must recognize that the kind of kinship one sees among AA members could to an extent exist among the well-controlled drinkers. People who have several drinks together on frequent occasions form business and other socioeconomic ties. Bacause of the inhibitions that alcoholic influence reduces, many business favors have been exchanged over the bar, whether the bar be a public one or in the home or office. Salesmen of large commodities feel they must entertain business clients with fairly copious amounts of liquor, and the influence of this liquor reduces sales resistance. As a matter of fact, more than one DWI suspect I have been involved with has been arrested after a big business powwow. In one instance the subject said, "How could such a wonderful meeting end in such a terrible insult as to be arrested for drunk driving?"

Obviously the more severe alcoholic will be carried away more so than the nonalcoholic, who has had only a few drinks. The big spender who tips the bartender fifty dollars can certainly award a contract to a drinking partner. Favors elicit favors, so perhaps there is a loosely knit alcoholic network. Theoretically, networks can exist between nondrinkers who abhor alcohol, but this may not be true nowadays as it might have been during the heyday of prohibitionists.

When the alcoholic finally decides on his own—and it must always be on his own—that his drinking has brought him more grief than anything else, he also realizes that he must give up the drinking culture. One alcoholic who came to me for a short while stated that he could not stop his drinking because people he associated with would not let him stop. He realized that he would have to give these people up as close friends, and he was not willing to do that. These people represented so much of his life that he would not give them up, too, so he kept on drinking and was subsequently arrested for drunkenness a few times before he attempted to abstain again. A few years later he was still drinking and adjusting to life marginally.

Chapter Thirteen
STARK REALITIES

IN SPITE of the nature of alcoholism and the terrible problem it is, popular literature, movies, and television tend to romanticize stories of alcoholics. This is understandable. They show how the alcoholic turns to the bottle for surcease from his many frustrations, then sinks to the point where he must live on the bottle for its own sake and finally, after just about reaching skid row he decides to turn about, often with the aid of friends, and comes back to live a better life than ever.

In real life this can happen, and the outcome is a worthy goal. However, one of the defects in this picture is that such stories emphasize the emotional and even "spiritual" agony of the alcohol addict without going into the nausea, pain, and other agonies of the physical body.

The intensity of frustration in having a mate who is generous in the barroom, setting up his friends, and perhaps the whole house, and then coming home with no money for his underfed and underclothed family is not a rare picture. Getting killed driving while drunk, or killing others, is also not rare, and certainly all these things evoke intense anger in others.

It is a fact that severely mentally ill people, especially chronic schizophrenics, become rejected by others because they are just plain filthy. They will not bathe or change clothes in many cases unless forced to. Excretory functions become great problems. This brings up a subject which is a most unpleasant one, and it is very applicable to alcoholism, because as with other conditions which tear down central nervous system functioning, physical neglect to the point of fecal and urinary incontinence is the lot of deteriorated alcoholics.

A case in point is one not in this series of 200, but one I was involved with, that of a sixty-two-year-old man with a woman of the same vintage, who was picked up for DWI. They were in an old car which was very neglected insofar as needed repairs were concerned; a real junk heap. When examined, the driver was found to be extremely filthy from head to foot, and the seat of his pants was wet from urinary incontinence. From their appearance, one could tell that they had been wet repeatedly. The odor was terrible. He was very intoxicated, with a blood alcohol level of 0.22 percent. During the examination, he said he was a man of great influence, and he would get the police in trouble for arresting him. He was from another state.

In a few other cases, I noted that suspects became incontinent during the examination. They seemed unaware of it, without any struggle to "hold it" or to go to the bathroom.

Urinary incontinence among drunks has long been a favorite subject for night club comedians, and the audience response seems to be at least as good as with the usual jokes about sex. One can think of anecdotes around this subject which seem very funny, partly because when incontinence occurs, especially when the subject is awake, his sensorium is in very poor shape. It is understandable that a person deeply asleep or in a coma with a full bladder will empty it automatically, but to be unaware or urinating or defecating while awake seems harder to believe.

It has often been said that when an alcoholic has poor urinary control, consistently, he has weak kidneys. Pathologic studies have shown that alcohol per se does not have a deleterious effect on the kidneys, or other parts of the genitourinary tract, such as might be the case with the liver or brain. It also has not been shown that alcohol deteriorates the spinal centers of urinary and fecal control specifically.

In the light of what is known about alcoholics who have developed poor urinary control, it might be concluded that it represents an extreme deterioration of self-awareness. It is a very marked "I don't care" attitude. Urologic conditions can complicate the picture, but in general it represents a regression to a very early psychosexual level which is seen in other forms of mental deterioration.

Philosophically, the extreme use of alcohol represents an expression of the death wish, or a death equivalent, a form of self-destruction which the drinker in vain tries to combine with euphoria. By the time excretory functions are ignored, or felt as pleasure, such as in wetting or playing with feces in bed, deterioration is extreme.

In rating disturbance of function to blood alcohol level, poor urinary control is often associated with a blood level near unconsciousness, over 0.3 percent. These figures may well be correct, but from experience one might conclude that it is the severely chronic alcoholic who fails by his deteriorated judgment to control his excretory needs.

How unpleasant it would be to live with such a filthy person is obvious. In my experience with cases of alcoholism it seems that when the alcoholic gets to the point of soiling himself, his wife decides to get rid of him, even if she is the kind of woman, due to certain unconscious needs, who marries one alcoholic after another. Apparently one who has a neurotic need to mother and/or dominate one who is weak and childlike, when wetting and soiling occur, finds that this is too much, and a total rejection occurs. It is almost like a dog lover who has his dog put to sleep when he starts making messes.

One might also conclude that once the alcoholic reaches the point of not caring whether he wets or soils himself, he needs institutional care whether he is motivated for it or not. By that time it may already be too late to save him, but we hate to give up. That such a person should be on the road as a driver is certainly not a question worthy of debate. No matter how the subject of self-destruction with alcohol can be romanticized in stories, the whole subject of extreme alcoholism can be classified as a filthy mess.

Chapter Fourteen

THE NATURE OF ALCOHOLISM

In chapter One we saw that the official definition of alcoholism emphasized control of intake. This would include alcoholics who are addicted to alcohol so that there is a physical and psychological craving overpowering all the time, and those who can go for lengths of time without drinking, yet drink very obsessively for limited periods. Other concepts include alcoholism as a defect in moral strength, a disturbance in social ability, or a symptom of an underlying mental illness.

A review of the literature on alcoholism reveals that real knowledge of the subject depends upon direct dealings with the people involved in it. However, such dealings are of limited value without some scientific knowledge as background.

Since alcoholism is a disease characterized by all sorts of faulty rationalizations and outright falsehoods, not only are personal observations plagued by inaccuracy, but many statistics are questionable in their meaning.

Alcoholism is indeed a unique subject, since it has many statistics applying to it, and yet at the same time there is still a tremendous amount of mystery surrounding it. Some of the statistics apparently contradict each other.

Through the years the world has seen a rather strange series of vague concepts. One might expect this, since we are dealing with a subject which does not lend itself to exactness in any phase of it, except insofar as chemistry and structural pathology are concerned. Even their contributions to the subject of alcoholism are quite limited.

The statistics you might have read about alcoholism probably consist of only a small fraction of those gathered through the years. Perhaps you know of some which would seem very pertinent in our discussion, but they are not gone into here in depth because through the years they have not provided very much help.

In relation to driving, we have seen an unusual opportunity to observe alcoholism and alcoholics. The situation is unique in that after an arrest involving erratic driving or an accident, there is a confrontation which is nonconforming to the denials of the arrested person. Arrests for drunkenness unrelated to driving might be similar in this respect, but the latter situation would apply to more extreme cases.

Obviously the drunk driver is in a position to cause more physical harm to others than he would in a nondriving situation, so the subject of drunk driving has rightly been the subject of many studies. Some of those of the past may be questionable in their relevance, since they tend to deal with known alcoholics and it has been shown that there are many more alcoholics than the known ones.

We have seen repeated proof that a hallmark of alcoholism is usually maximal denial. We might see this as denial of alcohol intake or the denial of problem drinking, admitting to only such things as social drinking or before dinner cocktails. One might really define an "occasional beer" as from one every two years to one every fifteen minutes. Obviously when a subject uses the term "occasional" he is trying to give the impression of having a drink no more often than once or twice every several days or more.

After reading the long chapter of sketchy case histories, which tend to illustrate certain points about the nature of alcoholism and the alcoholics' driving habits, a very burning question might come to your mind. How does it really feel to be an alcoholic? What is it like to live his life? Does an alcoholic think and feel basically as others do?

We have seen that the range of disorder insofar as how the mind works can go all the way from a very minor euphoria with slight impairment of judgment to a state wherein the alcoholic does not even know when he urinates or defecates. Somewhere between these extremes one might formulate a picture of what it is like to live the life of an alcoholic and how it really feels. Certainly it is not always a happy state of affairs, since the suicide rate among alcoholics is high. On the other hand, as we have seen, there are very strong positive feelings associated with it. Many alcoholics of several years' standing do not have any motivation to quit drinking, and they claim that they feel happy with their drinking habit. They would not want it any other way.

From what we have seen in the case histories, there is one thing we can say for certain, and that is that the picture is not a very simple one. Those of us who study the human mind know that the so-called normal brain functions are not simple, to say the least. To add the myriad of contradictions and distortions of alcohol would seem to complicate them further.

In the study of the normal human mind, Anna Freud found certain unconscious defense mechanisms, among which are repression, denial, reaction formation, intellectualization, displacement, and sublimation. These are mechanisms by which a person's unconscious mind, in order to meet certain deep needs, modifies and directs the conscious mind, helping the total organism to adjust to its environment and function productively, in a way which also satisfies the so-called rational needs of the mind.

The irrational, dreamlike unconscious mind is a tremendous foundation upon which the very rational or logical conscious mind is built. In the alcoholic these unconscious mechanisms, by drug inhibition of the higher functions, are laid bare in a way which at times is reminiscent of how the schizophrenic thinks, but there is a difference. The alcoholic can conform his expressions of the deeper levels of irrational thinking to what might be termed rational more skillfully than the psychotic can.

We might propose a principle at this point. The somewhat mild euphoria of alcohol, such as seen in the early stages of consumption, gives the whole world an optimistic appearance. One could venture to say that if a person were moody or depressed, having a small amount of alcohol could even improve judgment slightly to allow more creative or constructive thinking. Perhaps you have experienced this.

The next question coming to mind is whether the deeper problems of excessive drinking would be brought about by an extension or magnification of this mild euphoric state associated with small ingestions of alcohol, or whether there are other feelings motivating consumption of large amounts over a long period, which the average person has no insight into.

Although this is difficult to assess, perhaps we can reconsider some of the questions brought up before.

A very important thing we must take into consideration is the personality of the one who drinks heavily. Is he different to begin with than the person who drinks seldom or not at all? It would be a mistake to assume without reservation that he is, since it has never been actually proven that every person who develops alcoholism is always basically different than the person who does not, although it is widely believed among some experts that there is a real difference in personality to begin with. But on a scientific basis, this has not been proven. In other words, we must, in order to keep our minds open, consider the possibility that everyone has the potentiality of becoming an alcoholic, and there are certain chance factors in life directing the development of that state. Unfortunately, there are no experiments which have produced alcoholics from "normals." Experimentation has involved mainly the study of direct effects of alcohol on normal controls and alcoholics. The production of effects of alcohol over the years, on an experimental basis, would involve very altruistic and masochistic volunteers. Perhaps addiction could be produced, as in the case of other chemicals, on an experimental basis by giving subjects measured amounts of alcohol over a prolonged length of time. It is known that people who are forced to use habit forming narcotics because of physical conditions, regardless of underlying personalities, become addicted to them, and are subject to withdrawal symptoms after they are stopped. It has been postulated that the drug works itself into becoming a part of the metabolism of the individual, that it actually joins in the chemical structure of the cells, and that when it is withdrawn, collapse occurs. This is probably what happens in the case of delirium tremens, which can occur anywhere from a few hours to two weeks after the last drink. The body becomes universally irritable, and visual hallucinations, mainly of small animals, are the rule. It results in death in about 10 percent of cases. The basic chemistry of what really happens no one knows.

On the basis of past and present knowledge, it might be possible to form some picture of how addiction occurs.

There is a very old adage which I am sure you have heard. It probably sounds naive, because it goes back to the days long before much scientific knowledge was known. We realize that even in our present state of enlightenment a tremendous amount is not known about the subject.

The saying is this: *The man takes the drink. The drink takes the drink. The drink takes the man.*

The implication is that the man takes the drink for several reasons, curiosity only, or, usually, as a simple means of surcease from his trials in life. He is tired and tense. He just wants to unwind. He even feels a little frustrated, and a drink or two gives a restful euphoria. The euphoria is good, so he might want more. If he is well put together as an individual, a little relaxation is all that is necessary, since the rest of life has much in it for him. More drinks are unnecessary. He feels relaxed. He is not threatened by the feeling of the drinks wearing off. After a drink or two this should not be a big thing anyhow.

If he likes the effect, but feels an inner need for more, because, perhaps, there is little or no inner happiness, he takes more. The drink takes the drink.

After some inebriation, sleep can span the "going down" period. It he still cannot relax and, especially if he wants coma, a symbolic suicide, he drinks until sick, including nausea and vomiting, or until he passes out.

Usually this latter state of lack of control, which is the nature of alcoholism, takes years to develop. Judgment deteriorates as the drinking habit increases, and this contributes to the lack of control.

What inner feelings are involved? Certainly they include frustration and tiredness. The alcoholic euphoria is a definite change of feeling.

Alcohol has a toxic effect. It is a poisonous substance. Its poisonous effect in the early stage is expressed in some lack of judgment, delayed reaction time, etc. It has even been postulated recently that every drink of alcohol results in the loss of many brain cells.

The feelings involved during the inebriated state can at times be carried over to the sober times. Habit or conditioned reflex mechanisms can be involved here. There can be minor flashbacks of alcoholic euphoria while one is not under the influence. The dull, frustrating life enters in also, as a contrast.

All this can result in changes of value judgment, and attitudes, brought about during intoxication and carried over into the remainder of one's life. An "I don't care" attitude, everything rosy, etc. can persist, although the opposite can be true. Letdowns from alcoholic euphoria can result in deepening periods of depression during withdrawal and abstinence, becoming even a steady mood level. Usually the euphoria does not go into the nondrinking period, but many ways of thinking do, along with emotions such as despondency, irritability, hostility, impatience, or even unrealistic feelings of optimism.

Habit can change the alcoholic as it does anyone. Even in late life repeated actions or attitudes can gradually become a part of ones character. The need for euphoria increases especially because the individual is getting into more trouble and at times is suffering from rejection by loved ones. Alcohol then becomes a part of the biochemistry, and its need outweighs *every* other consideration. The drink takes the man. Preexisting moral principles, kindness, or consideration are of little importance.

This might answer in part the question of how an intelligent person, who realizes the terrible effect of drinking, can continue drinking heavily. He can profess lofty principles, but they mean little compared to deep needs. These deep needs certainly require very strong satisfactions on a conscious level to overcome them in a rehabilitation program.

The monumental work of Ralph S. Ryback, which represents the only thing really new and outstanding in research about alcohol, shows that there may not be as much difference between the occasional drinker's alcohol involvement and that of the heavy drinker as we have thought. I realize that this implies that this treatise contains a self-contradiction. However, it was proved that in all our investigated cases of DWI, alcoholism was definitely established.

However, Ryback proved that even in the absence of alcoholism, ingestion of more than very small amounts of alcohol produces measurable memory defects. These are probably not noticed in most cases by the subjects or their associates, but it is obvious in exaggerated form. Thus we find that to some extent the extreme mental aberrations of the severe alcoholic represent magnifications of memory and judgment defects detected in nonalcoholics drinking under experimental conditions. So even though in our series the person who drives erratically is a chronic alcoholic, any drinking affects driving somewhat.

Does this mean that any degree of alcoholic intake is a problem? Should everyone practice abstinence? But this confirms further that we are dealing with a very toxic substance. Alcohol dulls the mind whenever it is in the body and, over periods of time, it produces permanent pathologic changes.

Chapter Fifteen

HOW TO DEAL WITH THE PROBLEM?

Perhaps this study might have seemed "after the fact" in the light of recent publicity. During the preparation of this work several research projects have been suggested, because the problem has been recognized with more and more clarity. Perhaps the numbers of works in existence recently regarding this problem, including ones similar to this one, have prompted people to believe more firmly that the drunk driver is at least a "problem drinker" if not a full-blown alcoholic, and there has been a large public campaign to get such people off the road first, and then help them. Certainly the data we have gone over support this view very strongly. Actually there is no other way.

We have seen that even this way has its defects. Recently there was a statistic mentioned wherein even after losing their licenses, 80 percent of drivers "under suspension" are still on the road driving, taking their chances of getting caught. We have seen that because of their deterioration they are very impulsive, so that it is a very common thing for an alcoholic while drunk to care for nothing, say "To hell with it," and take the car out. How to stop this is a great problem indeed, and at times it may seem that the only way to do so would be to put the drunk driver in jail so that he could not possibly drive. Even jail does not seem to suffice. In some states, where drunk drivers are incarcerated, along with getting fines and license suspensions, their records do not seem to be much better than those wherein the penalty is less severe.

The biggest problem of all, as we have seen, is the fact that there really is no treatment for alcoholism without the alcoholic himself being inspired to get treatment. In other words, no matter how things are pushed upon a person, he will not be motivated until he wants to be. But perhaps the alcoholic who is suddenly faced with the loss of everything, including family and job, and whose only apparent

[71]

out is to kill himself, may give his life one more chance before he destroys himself completely. At times the alcoholic seems to realize that he cannot lick the problem, so he commits suicide. It is as if he is taking a little shortcut, since severe alcoholism is a sort of living death, which is more horrible than that which the horror movies show—zombies or dead bodies which are restless and moving around.

This sounds very hopeless, but in order to deal with the problem effectively there must be a facing of the true situation, and even though the proportion of complete rehabilitation is low, it seems worth the effort. The medical doctor who works with alcoholism can be compared to the neurosurgeon who operates on a lot of brain tumors, and even though perhaps four out of five patients are not really cured, the one saved by surgery makes the effort worthwhile. Those who are familiar with AA know that there are enough well, rehabilitated alcoholics, people who have gone as far as they could without losing their lives, who have stopped the drinking habit and are now living very profitable lives to make the efforts against alcoholism worth them. Even with cases of alcoholics who have abstained ten to fifteen years and have relapsed into drinking, one might say that the dry periods they had were worth the effort, and there is always more hope for the future.

Insofar as driving is concerned, the needs of the alcoholic must obviously be secondary to his potential victims. It is common practice to remove the driving privileges of mentally ill patients for long periods of time, until a psychiatrist can certify that he is emotionally fit to drive. [In my opinion, an alcoholic should not be allowed to drive until he has been dry long enough to recover good judgment, a year or more.]

There are some very optimistic and progressive suggestions as to how to bring chronic alcoholics into treatment, utilizing the DWI arrest. It is a requirement in some states that once a person has lost his license due to DWI there is a period of instruction followed by a test, after which a new license is issued with required insurance at a high risk premium. It has been proposed that during this driver reeducation, and afterwards, active treatment of alcoholism be a strict requirement.

The alcoholic must be treated for an extended period of time.

It must be remembered that when one is dealing with the alcoholic recently intoxicated or recently dried out, one is not communicating with a mind which has all its faculties. The alcoholic may be intact enough to sound very plausible, but it remains that we are dealing with a chronically poisoned brain which cannot be trusted completely. It needs continued support and guidance.

Alcohol is here to stay, but many people must be kept away from it. We know alcoholics can be rehabilitated. We can all do something about it.

TABLE I
JELLINEK'S PHASES OF ALCOHOL ADDICTION

	#—this series
Prodromal:	
1. Alcoholic palimpsests	
2. Surreptitious drinking	
3. Preoccupation with alcohol	
4. Avid drinking	
5. Guilt feelings about drinking behavior	
6. Avoid reference to alcohol	
7. Increasing frequency of "alcoholic palimpsests"	
Crucial:	
8. Loss of control	3
9. Rationalize drinking behavior	3
10. Social pressures	1
11. Grandiose behavior	1
12. Marked aggressive behavior	6
13. Persistent remorse	
14. Periods of total abstinence	4
15. Changing patterns of drinking	12
16. Drop friends	1
17. Quit jobs	4
18. Behavior becomes alcohol-centered	9
19. Loss of outside interests	7
20. Reinterpretation of interpersonal relations	1
21. Marked self pity	6
22. Geographic escape	4
23. Change in family habits	6
24. Unreasonable resentments	4
25. Protect supply	
26. Neglect of proper nutrition	1
27. First hospitalization	1
28. Decrease of the sexual drive	1
29. Alcoholic jealousy	4
30. Regular matutinal drinking	14
Chronic:	
31. Prolonged intoxication	7
32. Marked ethical deterioration	9
33. Impairment of thinking	9
34. Alcoholic psychoses	5
35. Drinks with persons far below social level	1
36. Takes recourse to "technical products"	
37. Loss of alcohol tolerance	15
38. Indefinable fears	4
39. Tremors	
40. Psychomotor inhibition	4
41. Drinking takes on obsessive character	19
42. Vague religious desires	1
43. Rationalization system fails	7

From *QJ Stud Alcohol*, 7:1-88, 1946.

TABLE II.
ANALYSIS OF RANDOM SERIES OF CASES

A. Sex (M or F)
B. Age at time of arrest
C. Previous arrests for DWI recorded in police files
D. Arrests for other offenses involving drunkenness
E. Arrests for offenses not definitely involving drunkenness
F. Reason for arrest:
    A = accident
    M = manner of operation
G. Degree of intoxication determined on examination
    0 = not intoxicated at all
    1 = mild
    2 = moderate
    3 = marked
H. Blood or equivalent urine level in %
I. Estimated phase of alcohol addiction—Jellinek scale
J. Admonition by judge (X)
K. Related diagnosis—cases having had treatment or counseling

	A	B	C	D	E	F	G	H	I	J	K
1.	M	45	2	1	8	M	3		41		
2.	M	24	2	7	0	M	3	.20	41	X	Neurotic conversion
3.	M	45	2	13	2	M	3	.18	42		Accident prone
4.	M	64	0	0	0	M	2	.16	31		
5.	F	47	0	0	0	M	2	.20	32		
6.	M	35	0	0	0	M	3	.21	41	X	
7.	M	33	1	0	0	M	2	.20	41	X	Neurotic anxiety
8.	M	46	0	0	0	A	2	.17	38		Neurotic depression
9.	M	67	1	0	2	M	2		40		Schizophrenia
10.	M	26	0	0	1	M	3		15	X	
11.	M	27	0	4	17	M	2	.35	34		
12.	M	39	2	1	2	M	2	.22			
13.	M	24	1	1	0	M	2	.28	32		
14.	M	25	0	0	0	M	2	.23	43	X	(Dead—cirrhosis)
15.	M	53	0	0	2	M	2	.20	28		
16.	F	52	0	0	0	M	2				
17.	M	46	0	0	0	M	2				

TABLE II.—Continued

	A	B	C	D	E	F	G	H	I	J	K
18.	M	42	0	0	0	M	2	.26	41	X	
19.	M	24	0	1	0	A	2	.14	33	X	
20.	M	37	1	7	2	M	2	.22	19	X	
21.	M	51	0	0	0	M	2	.19	37		
22.	M	32	0	0	0	M	2	.20	31	X	
23.	M	30	0	0	0	M	2	.24	37		
24.	M	56	0	0	0	M	2	.18	41		
25.	M	38	0	0	0	A	2	.17	30		
26.	M	56	1	1	0	A	2	.22	31		
27.	M	27	1	0	14	M	1	.16	11		
28.	M	25	1	1	2	A	1	.17	30		
29.	M	41	0	0	2	M	2	.20	37		
30.	M	25	2	0	0	A	2	.16	18		
31.	M	22	2	0	0	M	3	.18	33		
32.	M	41	0	1	5	M	2	.21	30		
33.	M	27	1	5	2	M	3	.24	19		
34.	M	23	1	1	3	M	3	.17	34		
35.	M	25	0	1	4	A	3		33		
36.	M	48	1	5	0	M	2	.26	18		
37.	M	44	0	0	0	M	2	.17	22		
38.	M	23	0	0	0	M	2	.16	21		
39.	M	49	0	0	0	M	0	.06	9		
40.	M	18	0	0	0	M	2	.17	24		(suicide attempt)
41.	M	38	0	0	0	*A	2	.10	8		Neurotic depression
42.	M	19	0	2	0	M	2	.17	29		
43.	M	32	0	0	0	A	3		43		
44.	M	43	0	0	0	A	3		35		
45.	M	42	0	0	6	M	1	.12	15		
46.	M	25	0	1	4	M	2	.20	15	X	Impotency
47.	M	37	2	1	0	M	3	.22	32	X	
48.	M	34	0	1	0	M	2	.16	8		
49.	M	19	0	0	0	M	3	.20	26		
50.	M	51	0	0	0	M	2	.18	15		
51.	M	32	0	0	0	M	2	.20	21		
52.	M	33	0	0	0	M	2				

How to Deal With the Problem

[Table of data — columns appear to include case number, sex (M/F), age, and various numerical measures, with diagnostic categories marked with X]

#	Sex	Age								Dx
53.	M	50	0	0	0	A	0	.01	32	"Psychosomatic"
54.	F	24	0	0	0	M	3	.24		
55.	M	43	3	0	0	M	2	.24	15	
56.	M	33	1	0	6	M	2	.21		
57.	M	36	1	0	0	M	2	.19	23	
58.	M	49	0	0	0	M	3	.16	37	X
59.	M	38	0	0	1	A	3	.22	41	
60.	F	66	0	0	0	M	2	.24	30	
61.	M	42	0	4	2	A	3	.17	10	
62.	M	31	0	1	0	M	2	.23	18	
63.	M	43	3	0	2	M	2	.22		Neurosis, mixed
64.	M	21	0	0	0	M	1	.21	38	Homosexual
65.	M	55	3	0	0	M	2	.18	41	
66.	M	31	0	0	0	M	2	.20	37	
67.	M	36	1	0	0	M	2	.28	14	
68.	M	26	0	1	1	A	1		9	Neurotic depression
69.	M	21	0	0	0	M	2	.12	43	
70.	M	45	0	2	0	M	2	.16	19	
71.	M	49	2	0	1	M	2	.22		
72.	M	35	0	0	0	M	2	.21	23	Schizophrenia
73.	M	21	0	0	0	M	1	.16	17	
74.	M	22	0	0	1	M	2	.14		X
75.	M	23	0	1	1	M	1	.18	41	
76.	M	25	0	0	0	M	2	.12	41	
77.	M	47	0	0	0	M	1	.25	33	
78.	M	45	0	9	0	M	3	.24	32	Impotency
79.	M	33	0	0	0	M	3		12	X
80.	M	30	0	0	1	M	2	.22	40	
81.	M	21	0	1	0	A	2	.13	30	Epileptic
82.	M	27	0	2	2	M	2		15	X
83.	M	27	0	1	0	M	2		30	
84.	M	29	0	0	1	A	2	.20	37	
85.	M	44	2	3	3	M	2	.20	19	"Functional pain"
86.	M	56	0	0	0	M	3	.28	41	X
87.	M	33	1	0	1	M	2	.26	18	
88.	M	52	0	0	1	M	2		*31	
89.	M	45	0	0	1	M	2			
90.	M	26	0	0	1	M	3			

*Committed upon arrest

TABLE II.—Continued

	A	B	C	D	E	F	G	H	I	J	K
91.	M	27	0	1	0	A	2	.28	38	X	Neurotic depression
92.	M	24	0	3	1	M	3		29	X	Neurotic depression
93.	M	59	0	0	0	M	2	.18	31		Dead—Ca. rectum
94.	M	23	0	0	0	M	3	.28	30		
95.	M	21	0	0	0	A	2	.21	18		Neurotic anxiety
96.	M	51	2	0	2	M	1	.21	43		
97.	M	22	0	0	0	M	2	.17	30		
98.	M	22	0	1	0	M	2	.20	24	X	
99.	M	47	0	0	0	M	2	.18	23		
100.	M	35	0	0	1	M	2	.22	15		
101.	M	20	0	0	0	A	2	.22	41	X	Cirrhosis
102.	M	27	2	8	5	A	3		34		
103.	M	38	1	17	6	M	2	.16	37		
104.	F	42	0	0	0	M	2	.24	32		
105.	M	49	1	0	0	M	2	.25	30		
106.	M	23	0	0	1	M	1	.14	12		
107.	M	26	0	0	0	M	3	.22	34	X	
108.	M	28	0	0	0	M	2		21		
109.	M	28	1	0	7	M	2	.20	29		
110.	M	26	2	2	2	M	0		15		
111.	M	53	0	2	1	M	2		40	X	
112.	M	21	1	2	0	M	2	.13	30	X	Schizophrenia
113.	M	18	1	0	2	M	2	.17	33	X	
114.	M	31	0	0	12	M	2	.18	37		
115.	M	31	0	1	1	M	2	.17	22		
116.	M	39	3	9	21	M	2		21		
117.	M	25	0	0	0	M	2	.16	12		Accident prone
118.	M	25	0	0	1	M	2	.24	23		
119.	M	19	0	0	0	A	2	.19	41		
120.	M	41	0	7	5	M	3	.24	37		
121.	M	52	0	1	5	M	3		33		Homicide
122.	M	35	0	0	0	M	2	.21			Chronic gastritis
123.	M	61	0	0	0	M	8	.28			
124.	M	20	0	0	0	A	2				
125.	M	35	0	0	0	M	1	.16			

How to Deal With the Problem

126.	M	23	1	1	4	M	2	.17	24	Multiple accidents
127.	M	20	0	0	0	M	2	.**16**		
128.	M	60	0	0	0	M	2	.17		
129.	M	17	0	0	0	A	1	.12	12	
130.	M	31	2	0	2	M	3	.24	18	
131.	M	29	0	1	0	A	2		12	
132.	M	27	0	2	0	M	2	.14	15	
133.	M	26	1	2	0	A	1	.12	8	
134.	M	26	1	1	0	M	2	.17	17	
135.	M	25	0	2	9	M	1		17	
136.	M	48	1	2	0	M	3		41	Indecent exposure
137.	M	20	0	2	2	A	1	.16	41	Gastric ulcer
138.	M	21	1	0	0	M	2	.23	37	
139.	M	24	0	1	1	M	2	.18	19	
140.	M	43	1	1	0	M	2	.23	21	
141.	M	59	0	0	0	M	2	.12	14	
142.	M	23	0	0	0	M	3	.28	43	Schizophrenia
143.	M	64	0	0	0	A	2	.13	41	Dyamenorrhea
144.	M	23	0	0	1	A	1	.14	41	Sociopathic
145.	M	30	0	0	0	A	2	.20	18	
146.	M	43	0	1	1	A	2		19	
147.	F	22	0	1	0	A	2	.17	15	
148.	M	19	0	0	1	A	2	.18		X
149.	M	52	1	0	0	M	1	.18	16	
150.	M	19	0	1	2	A	1	.16	17	
151.	M	22	0	0	0	A	1	.18		
152.	M	25	0	0	0	A	2	.16	19	Gastric ulcer
153.	M	24	0	0	0	M	2	.24	21	Neurotic depression
154.	M	44	0	0	0	A	2	.16	32	3 auto accidents
155.	M	41	0	4	0	M	2	.15	24	
156.	M	21	1	0	1	A	3	.36	43	
157.	M	45	1	1	13	A	3	.27	31	
158.	M	24	1	1	0	M	3	.20	30	
159.	M	28	0	0	0	A	3	.22	40	
160.	M	27	0	0	0	A	2	.17	21	
161.	M	21	0	0	0	M	3	.25	37	Neurotic depression
162.	M	59	0	0	9	A	3	.24	41	
163.	M	66	1	1	9	A	3			

TABLE II.—Continued

	A	B	C	D	E	F	G	H	I	J	K
164.	M	41	1	7	12	M	2				
165.	M	22	0	0	1	M	1	.13	34		
166.	M	46	2	0	1	M	3		31		
167.	M	25	0	1	0	M	2	.12	30		
168.	M	57	2	3	0	M	2		34		
169.	M	68	1	1	2	M	2				
170.	M	27	0	0	0	A	2	.15			
171.	M	23	0	0	0	M	1				
172.	M	20	2	3	0	M	3	.10	30		
173.	M	31	3	9	14	A	2	.26			Personality disorder
174.	M	57	0	1	0	M	3	.22	37		
175.	M	36	0	0	8	A	2	.16	22		Sexual psychopath
176.	M	44	4	1	0	M	3		15		
177.	M	21	0	0	1	A	0	.06	14		
178.	M	41	0	0	0	M	2	.20	18		
179.	M	23	0	1	8	M	2	.18	12		
180.	M	24	1	1	4	M	2	.22	38		Personality disorder
181.	M	22	1	0	0	M	2	.24	23		Neurotic anxiety
182.	M	50	0	0	16	M	2	.16	23		
183.	M	49	0	1	1	A	2	.17	22		
184.	M	19	0	0	0	M	0	.02			
185.	M	32	0	2	3	A	3	.20	27		
186.	M	33	2	1	0	M	2		37		
187.	M	22	0	0	21	A	2		20		
188.	M	18	0	0	0	A	2	.10	14		
189.	F	41	0	0	2	A	2	.20	18		
190.	F	35	0	2	2	A	2	.15	37		Neurotic depression
191.	M	19	0	0	0	A	2	.17	9		
192.	M	21	0	0	12	M	2	.26	32		
193.	M	23	0	2	0	M	2	.18	15		
194.	M	47	0	0	0	A	2	.23			
195.	M	37	3	13	3	M	3	.21	29		
196.	M	37	0	0	5	M	3		33		
197.	M	49	0	1	0	A	3	.22	32		
198.	M	23	0	0	0	M	2	.17	30		
199.	M	58	0	1	0	A	3	.28	33		Neurotic depression
200.	M	49	0	0	0	A	1	.24	43		

BIBLIOGRAPHY

1. Jellinek, E. M.: Phases in the drinking history of alcoholics. *Q J Stud Alcohol,* 7:1-88, 1946.
2. Ryback, R. S.: Blackouts are evaluated in nonalcoholics. *Recovery,* 4 (No. 4:1, 1970.
3. Selzer, M. L.: The alcoholic driver: myth or menace? *Psychiat Opinion,* 6: 11-15, 1969.

INDEX

A

Abuse, drug, 54
Accident vs. manner of operation, 11
Addiction, alcoholic, 61, 67
Age, 11
Alcoholic addition, 67, 68
Alcoholics Anonymous, 7
Alcoholism, 64, 65, 66, 68
   definition, 4
   past beliefs, 3
   treatment, 71
Amphetamines, 55, 56
Appeals, 10
Assault, 12

B

Barbiturates, 56
Blackouts, 15, 16
Blankouts, 15, 16
Blood alcohol level, 9, 11

C

Car pools, 52
Cerebellar signs, 9
Character disorders, 44
Chlorpromazine, 54
Clinical records, 13
Coin test, 9
Conscious mind, 66
Contradictions, 16
Coordination, 3

D

Death, symbolic, 72
Defense mechanims, 66
Delirium tremens, 19, 67
Denial, 16, 17, 35, 65
Depression, 49, 69
Deterioration, 40
Drug abuse, 54
Drying out, 19

E

Euphoria, 18, 66, 68, 69
Excretory functions, 61
Eye signs, 8

F

Fecal Incontinence, 62, 63
Female vs. male, 11
Finger to nose test, 9
Freud, Anna, 66

G

Gait, 9

H

Habit, 69

I

Illness, mental, 35, 36, 42, 43
Incontinence, fecal, 62, 63
Incontinence, urinary, 62, 63
Interpersonal relationships, 57
Interviews, method of, 8

J

Jellinek scale, 15
Judgment, 16

L

License supension, 46, 71

M

Male vs. female, 11
Manner of operation vs. accident, 11
Marijuana, 55
Mental illness, 35, 36, 42, 43
Mechanisms of defense, 66

[83]

Memory defects, 15, 16, 70
Metabolism of alcohol, 10
Mind, conscious, 66
Mind, unconscious, 66
Mood swings, 6

P

Palimpsests, 15
Paraldehyde, 54
Personality, alcoholic, 67
Personality, sociopathic, 44, 45
Progression of disease, 18
Prohibitionists, 58
Projection, 13
Psychedelics, 57
Psychiatric problems, 7
Psychopaths, 44
Psychotherapy, 43
Public transportation, 52
Pupil changes, 9

R

Reaction time, 3
Records, clinical, 13
Rehabilitation, 72, 73
Relationships, interpersonal, 57
Relatives of alcoholics, 12

Romberg test, 9
Ryback, Ralph S., 69

S

Schizophrenia, 7, 46, 61
Sedatives, 56
Sedativisim, 36
Seltzer, M. L., 6
Slurring of speech, 8
Sociopathic personality, 44, 45
Sources of information, 12
Speech, 18
Suicide, 72
Suspension of driving, 71

T

Thorazine, 54
Tolerance to alcohol, 10
Toxicity of alcohol, 68
Tranquilizers, 56
Transportation, public, 52
Treatment of alcoholism, 71

U

Unconscious mind, 66
Urinary incontinence, 62, 63

NO LONGER THE PROPERTY
OF THE
UNIVERSITY OF R.I. LIBRARY